D1071011

It's Fun to Know Why

IT'S FUN

TO KNOW WHY

EXPERIMENTS WITH THINGS AROUND US

BY JULIUS SCHWARTZ

Illustrated by Edwin Herron

WHITTLESEY HOUSE

McGRAW-HILL BOOK COMPANY, INC.

New York London Toronto

IT'S FUN TO KNOW WHY

Library of Congress Catalog Card Number: 51-13609

Published by Whittlesey House
A division of the McGraw-Hill Book Company, Inc.
Printed in the United States of America

Contents

It's Fun to Know Why

Adventure and Discovery

This is a book of adventure and discovery. Yet you will not have to travel to far-off lands or visit strange places. Many curious and exciting things may be found right around you in ordinary, everyday stuff like iron and coal, bread and salt, paper and glass. You can be the explorer and make the discoveries. You are the hero of this book!

You can make these discoveries by using your eyes and your hands. You can experiment to find out:

how wood is changed into coal
how iron turns to rust
how to get salt out of sea water
why bread is full of holes
why a magnifying glass magnifies
why soap cleans

You can see many things that you have not noticed before:

shining crystals shaped like ice cubes in a pinch of salt
thousands of plant fibers in a piece of newspaper
glittering specks of colored glass in a handful of sand
white flour in a single wheat seed

You can make real paper; you can make bread from seeds; you can make things from rubber and cement; you can make a loom and weave cloth on it.

You will see how adventurous people of the past discovered precious materials in rocks and soil, in plants and animals, and in the waters of the ocean. You will understand how they changed these materials into the many useful things that you see around you.

All this and much more too! Best of all, you will not need special scientific instruments for your adventures. Most of the things are around your house now, and your home will be your workshop.

Start your explorations!

Iron—King of the Metals

IRON IN YOUR HOUSE

How would you like to be a detective? Here is your job: find all the things in your house that have iron in them.

All you need for this detective work is a pencil and paper and an "iron detector." Can you guess what an "iron detector" is? Just an ordinary magnet! If you have ever experimented with a magnet, you have probably discovered that it can pick up small iron things and that it is pulled toward larger iron objects.

Start your hunt in the kitchen. Bring your magnet near any "suspicious" thing, like a steampipe or a stove. Is your magnet pulled toward it? Do you have to pull in order to get it away? If so, there is iron present. Write down the name of each iron object you find. Continue your hunt to the other rooms of your house. How long is your list? Have you forgotten anything, like a carpet tack or a garbage can? Perhaps you should explore your house a second time. Now how long is your list?

Many of the things on your list are made of a special kind of iron called steel. You will find out more about steel later. But first, examine your list carefully. As a good detective, you will want to explain why iron is found in so many things in your house. Here are a few clues:

The carving knife is sharp, and it can bend without breaking.
The top of the kitchen table is thin and flat, but strong.
The paper clip is springy.
The head of your hammer can be banged hard against many things without cracking.

Detective, what is your conclusion? Have you found that iron things can be strong, springy, sharp, and hard? Have you also found that iron can be made into many shapes—flat sheets, hollow tubes, twisted springs, or solid bars? Then you are right!

Whether it is a tack or a hammer, a hairpin or a fire escape, iron does its job. No wonder it is called the king of the metals.

WHERE IRON COMES FROM

If you could travel to northern Minnesota, you would come to a place known as the Mesabi (mee-sah′-bee) range. Here you would find the largest iron mine in the world. As you approached the mine you would notice the red earth underneath your feet. This red earth doesn't look like iron at all, but it is the stuff from which we get iron. It is iron ore. You would watch giant electric shovels scooping as much as 14 tons of this iron ore from the open ground in each huge bite. Then you would see the shovels swing around and drop their load of ore into waiting freight cars.

Even if you cannot travel to an iron mine, you can still see something very much like iron ore right where you live. It may surprise you to know that the red rust which is sometimes found on iron things is the same kind of material as the iron ore which is dug out of the Mesabi mines. Would you like to make some of this ore?

You Will Need:

2 new pieces of steel wool
a bowl
a pair of gloves
a blotter
a dish to cover the bowl

Put on your gloves to protect your fingers. Wet the blotter and place it in the bottom of the bowl. Now rub the two pieces of steel wool against each other so that small shreds of it fall all over the wet blotter.

Cover the bowl with a dish so that the blotter will not dry out. Look at the steel wool every half hour. What is happening? Is the steel changing into rust? You have made the iron in it change back into iron ore!

How can iron turn to rust? Chemists tell us that when iron is in moist air, it joins with the oxygen in the air to make something entirely new. You call this new thing rust. The miner calls it iron ore. The chemist calls it iron oxide.

CHANGING IRON ORE INTO IRON

How is the red iron ore which is dug out of the mines changed into useful iron? You have just learned that iron ore is made of iron *joined* with oxygen. To get the iron out of the ore, then, we have to get rid of the oxygen.

This is done in huge furnaces called blast furnaces. Iron ore is fed into the top of the furnace. Coke (a kind of roasted coal) is then dumped on top of the iron ore. As the hot coke burns, it takes the oxygen away from the iron ore. When the ore loses its oxygen, it becomes iron.

Every six hours the melted iron is allowed to run out of an opening in the bottom of the blast furnace into waiting containers.

PIG IRON AND STEEL

The iron made in blast furnaces is called pig iron. It can be used in different ways. Sometimes it is poured into molds. Here the iron hardens and takes the shape of the mold, in the same way that gelatin does in a cup. Lamp posts, pipes, steam radiators are made in this way. So are bathtubs and washbasins, but these are covered with white porcelain. When pig iron is used in this way it is called cast iron. Most of the pig iron, however, is used for the making of steel.

To make steel it is necessary to change the pig iron into a purer kind of iron. Pig iron has carbon and other chemicals mixed in with it. These chemicals make pig iron brittle. A heavy blow to a bathtub made of pig iron will make it crack. To change brittle pig iron into tough steel, we must burn out most of these unwanted chemicals. This is done by reheating the pig iron in a large furnace called a Bessemer furnace. The hot, melted steel which is poured out of this furnace now contains only iron and a small amount of carbon. It is much stronger than pig iron.

The steel is allowed to harden and is then sent to the finishing mills. Here it is heated white hot. Then any of a number of things are done to it. It may be rolled, pressed, squeezed, cut, drawn, cast, or hammered into its finished shape. Then it is ready to be used to make tractors and steam shovels, automobiles and airplanes, locomotives and rails, skyscrapers and bridges, and all the other things that make our times known as the "Age of Steel."

THE KING'S SICKNESS

Although iron is the king of the metals, it has one serious weakness—it rusts. You discovered this weakness when you saw your steel wool crumbling into red, flaky rust. But just as man has learned how to prevent human diseases, so has he found ways of preventing this rusting disease of iron. Would you like to try some of these ways?

You Will Need:

6 clean iron nails
a piece of cardboard
fingernail polish
machine oil
any oil paint
aluminum paint (if you happen to have some handy)
a bowl
a plate to cover the bowl
a wad of cotton

Stand the six nails upright by pushing them part way into the cardboard. Now they are ready for the treatment. Paint one of the nails with some fingernail polish. Smear machine oil on another nail. Paint a third nail with any oil paint. Paint the fourth with aluminum paint. Don't treat the last two nails at all.

Now line the bowl with soaking wet cotton. When all the nails are dry, place them in their cotton beds. Cover the bowl with the plate. Look at the nails the next day. How are they getting along? Which are sick with rust? Which are not? You have discovered how to prevent the rusting disease of iron!

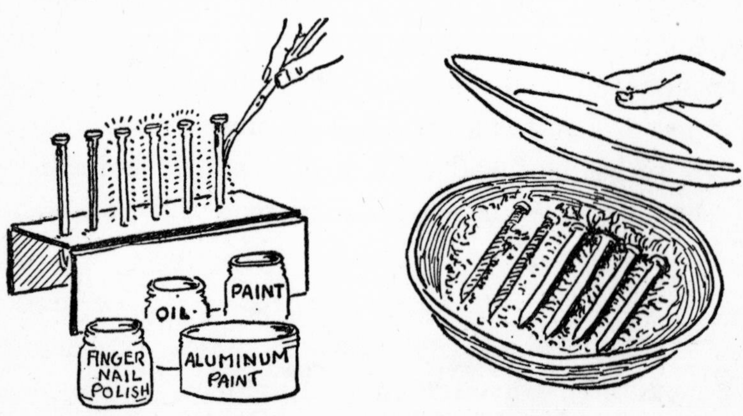

You have found that iron rusts when it is open to moisture and air. You have also found that anything which can keep the moisture and the air away from the iron will prevent this rusting disease. Now you can understand why:

Oil is smeared on tools after they have been used in the garden.

Radiators and pipes are painted.

Garbage cans are made of iron which has been coated with another metal called zinc.

Iron bathtubs are covered with porcelain.

"Tin" food cans are really made of steel which has been coated with a thin covering of tin.

Stainless-steel kitchen knives are made of steel mixed with metals like chromium and nickel. These metals prevent oxygen from rusting the steel.

IRON FROM THE SKIES

People long ago used to call iron the "metal from heaven." There was a good reason for this. They did not know that the crumbling iron ore in the ground underneath them could be changed into hard, solid iron. But they did know about one kind of iron—the kind that they found when a "shooting star" landed on the earth.

Have you ever seen a shooting star flash across the sky at night? These are not really stars at all. They are small pieces of rocky stuff which come from the space far outside the earth. Most of these rocks, or meteors, as they are called, crumble into dust as they streak through the air high above the earth. Now and then, however, one of these meteors lands on the earth. These rocks have a large amount of hard iron in them. This was the only iron that the people of olden times knew about. This was their "metal from heaven."

Coal – Black Diamonds

Have you ever seen coal burning in a stove or in a large furnace? Have you watched the flickering yellow and blue flames dancing above the coal? Have you felt a warm glow on your face? Have you wondered where all this black stuff comes from?

WHERE COAL COMES FROM

You know that trucks deliver coal to houses. You know that the trucks picked up their loads at a coalyard. You know that the coal was brought to the coalyard by freight train or coal barge from a coal mine many miles away. But do you know how the coal got into the mine?

Miners digging deep into the earth for coal often find the markings of leaves, stems, and roots of plants on

slabs of coal. Scientists, looking closely at thin pieces of coal under a magnifying microscope, often find the same tiny structures in the coal as they do in trees.

Coal was once wood. This may seem strange to you, because you know that when trees die and fall to the ground, they break up into tiny pieces and help form the soil in which new plants will grow. The plants which formed coal, however, did *not* rot in this way. Then what did happen to them?

Scientists have studied coal mines carefully, trying to figure out just what happened to these trees. This is the story that they tell us. Some 250,000,000 years ago certain parts of the earth, like the place that is now Pennsylvania, were huge swamplands. Dense forests grew in the wet soils of these swamps. When the trees in these forests died, they fell into the swamp water. In these waters the dead trees did not rot. Later they were covered by mud and sand.

But how was the buried wood changed into coal? It will be easier for you to understand the answer that scientists give to this question if you do this experiment:

You Will Need:

- 2 wooden toothpicks (or any other small clean sticks)
- a piece of paper
- a metal pie plate

Place the sticks in the pie plate. Heat them on your kitchen stove. Notice the smoky gas coming from the heated wood. What is happening to the wood? Do you see it turning brown and then black? When all your sticks have become black, turn the heat off. *Wait at least five minutes* for the pie plate to cool. Take out a stick and with it write the word CHARCOAL on a piece of paper, because this is what you have made.

By heating wood, you changed it into charcoal. The heat boiled the water and some other materials out of the wood. These things went up in the smoke. The charcoal that was left in the plate was made mostly of black carbon.

Scientists believe that the coal that we dig out of our mines was made in very much the same way that your charcoal was. Two things helped in changing the buried wood into coal—heating and squeezing. Deep under the earth it is very hot. This earth heat did the same thing to the buried wood that your oven heat did to your sticks. It boiled the water and the other materials out of the wood. What was left was mostly black carbon—coal. Squeezing helped, too. You remember that the wood was buried under mud and sand. This heavy load pressed hard on the buried wood and helped in squeezing the water and other materials out of it. After many, many thousands of years of heating and squeezing, the buried wood became coal.

COAL OF DIFFERENT KINDS AND SIZES

After coal is dug out of the mine it is broken and sorted into different sizes. Each size has its own name. Here are some of them: lump, egg, stove, chestnut, pea, buckwheat, and boiler. Each kind of stove or furnace works best when it has the right size of coal in it.

You have probably heard about two kinds of coal that are very useful, soft coal and hard coal. Soft coal has less carbon in it than hard coal. It burns with a smoky flame and often fills the air with soot. Nevertheless it is very useful, especially in large factories, because it is plentiful and it is cheap. Some of the factories that burn soft coal are experimenting to see if they can trap all of the soot before it escapes from the chimney.

Hard coal is more expensive than soft coal, but it burns with an almost smokeless flame and leaves little ash. This kind of coal is excellent for heating homes. Hard coal is harder than soft coal because it was given an extra hard squeeze by the rocks in the earth while it was forming.

BURNING COAL

The next time you have a chance to see a coal furnace, look at it carefully. Of course the most interesting thing about it is the burning coal. This burning coal sits on an iron grate. As the coal burns, some of the ashes fall through the grate to the ashpit below. The rest of the ashes are made to fall into the ashpit by shaking the grate with a special handle.

Now look at some of the doors on the furnace. First there is the door that opens into the place where the coal is burning. This is the door which we open when we want to throw more coal on the fire. Then there is a lower door, which allows us to shovel the ashes out of the ashpit.

But these doors, and one more that you may see on the side of the furnace, have another job. You can find out what this job is by doing an experiment. Instead of using coal, you are going to use a candle. Instead of a furnace, you are going to use a saucer and a jar.

You Will Need:

- a kitchen sink (because this is where you do the experiment)
- a birthday candle
- a glass jar
- a saucer

Place the saucer in the sink. Hold a lighted match under the bottom of the candle for a few seconds. Blow out the match and then press the candle to the saucer to make it stick. Now light the candle. Place the jar, mouth down, over the candle. What happens? The candle burns for a short time, and then flickers and goes out.

Now lift your jar from the saucer and shake it for about a minute to get rid of all the smoke. Then light the candle again. Place your jar over it as you did before. This time, however, try to save the flickering light by lifting the jar a few inches. Does the candle continue to burn?

The candle went out the first time because there was no opening for fresh air to come in. The candle kept on burning the second time because you made an opening for the fresh air.

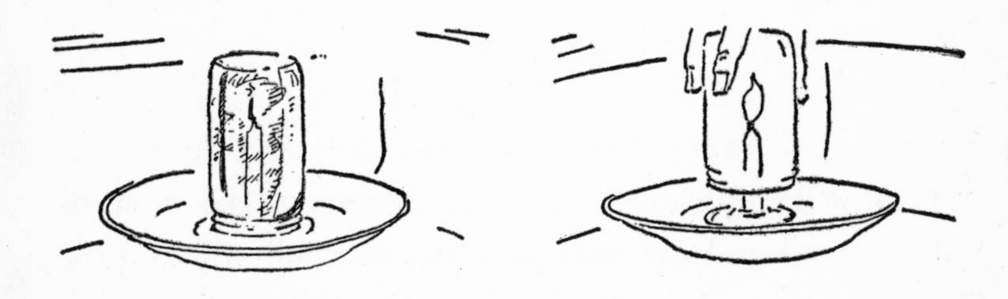

A candle needs a fresh supply of air if it is to burn. And so does the coal in a furnace. This fresh supply comes through openings in the furnace doors. If you look carefully at the large furnace doors you will notice that they have little sliding doors in them. These sliding doors can be moved to allow more or less air to come into the furnace.

Something else helps too. You remember that you had to shake the jar after the first experiment, to get rid of the smoke. We can get rid of the smoke from a furnace in an easier way. If you look at the top of a furnace you will see a large pipe, the chimney, which carries smoke safely out of the building.

FROM COAL TO TELEVISION

Man has made good use of the rich store of coal which nature has buried in the earth. Coal is very important to man because it is plentiful and because it is a wonderful heatmaker. Long ago, coal was burned only in open fireplaces or in stoves to supply the heat that was needed in homes and factories. Nowadays, we often use the heat from burning coal in a roundabout way.

First the coal fire is placed under a boiler of water. The heat from the fire changes the water into steam. Then the hot steam that comes out of the boiler is made to do many useful jobs for us. In many houses it rises into radiators to warm the rooms. In a locomotive it pushes against pistons and makes the wheels turn. In a generating station it spins the blades of steam turbines to make electricity for a town or city. This electricity lights homes, heats toasters, chills refrigerators, runs washing machines, and makes pictures on television screens. And all of this comes from the heat of burning coal.

TREASURES FROM COAL

In the chapter on iron, we learned about a special kind of roasted coal—coke. You remember that coke helped in changing iron ore into iron. What is coke? How is it made? Coke is made by roasting soft coal in special ovens. Here the coal does not burn. Instead, it turns into a light, silvery-gray material called coke. Coke burns at a higher temperature than soft coal. It can make the fiercely hot temperatures that are needed in the making of iron.

In the past, coke was made in round ovens called "beehive ovens." The heated coal in these ovens gave off a bad-smelling smoke, something like the smoke that you made in your charcoal experiment. This smoke was allowed to escape into the air. Later it was found that there was a useful, burnable gas in this smoke. This coal gas is now trapped in large tanks and is then piped to homes to be used in kitchen ranges or gas heaters.

But there was another treasure in the smoke from coke ovens. This was a brown, sticky tar. Scientists have learned how to make thousands of wonderful things from this coal tar. Here are a few of them:

Aspirin, for the relief of pain
Dyes of every color of the rainbow
Explosives like TNT
Naphthalene, the stuff in mothballs
Perfumes, to make hundreds of sweet smells
Pitch, for tar paper and asphalt streets
Plastics, like Bakelite
Saccharin, which is 500 times as sweet as sugar
Sulfa drugs, to fight the bacteria of disease

No wonder coal is often called "black diamonds."

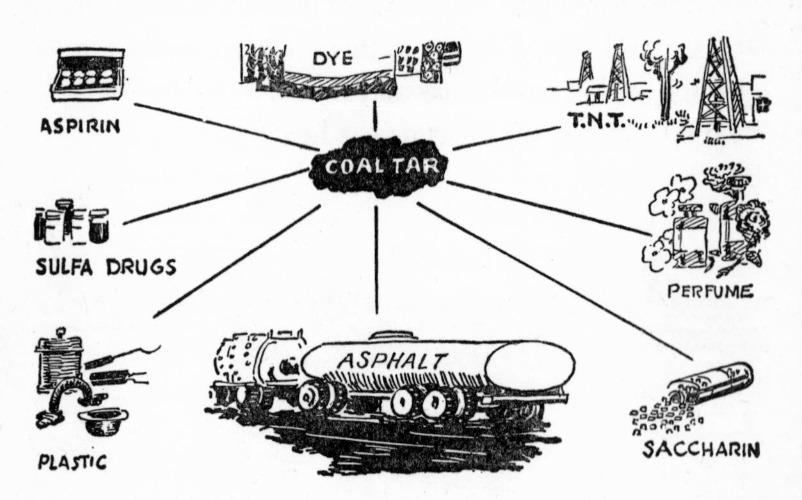

Cement–Rock of Ages

A few years ago the newspapers and magazines told the story of how a builder was making houses in a new way. He poured them! First he moved a large boxlike steel form to the place where the house was to be built. Then cement mixers poured their churned-up mixture of sand, gravel, cement, and water into the spaces between the inner and outer walls of the steel forms. In a few days the mixture hardened into stonelike concrete. The steel forms were then taken down. Except for the roof, the house was all built before a nail was driven. The builder then moved the form to another place and poured another house.

MAKE IT FROM CONCRETE

You have probably watched men working in your own neighborhood, opening bags of cement and mixing the gray powder in them with sand, gravel, and water. You saw them dump this mixture between wooden forms. If you came back in a few days you found that the wooden forms had been taken down and that solid concrete was left.

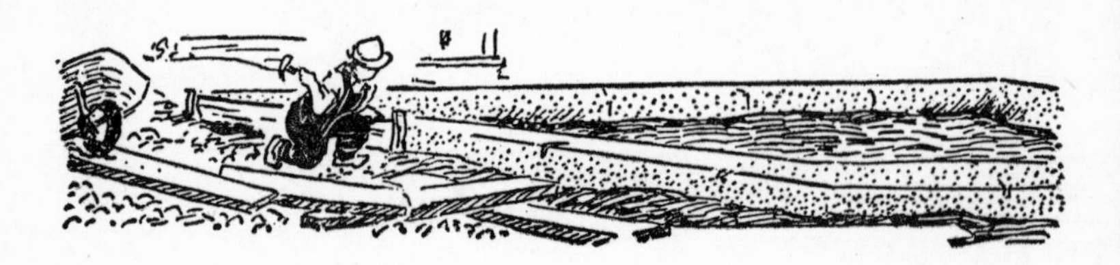

How would you like to make something out of concrete? Here's the way to make a useful paperweight–pencil holder for your desk:

You Will Need:

- a small amount of Portland cement (about ½ pound)
- a small bag of sand (the sand should be coarse, not fine)
- water
- a knife
- oil (any kind)
- a tin pie plate
- an old spoon (for mixing)
- a tablespoon
- an empty milk carton
- a nail
- 4 pencils
- newspaper (spread this under all your work, so that you do not mess up the kitchen)

1. Making the Form

Cut through the milk carton about 4 inches above the bottom to make the small box which is going to hold the concrete. Make a cover for this box by cutting a piece of cardboard from the other part of the carton. Make the cover just a little bit larger than the top of the box, so that it doesn't fall in. This cover is going to hold the pencils in the concrete while it is drying. Punch four holes in the cover with a nail. Push the pencils through these holes.

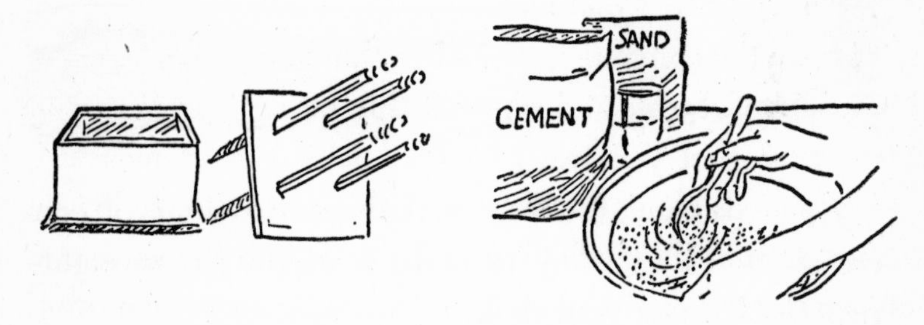

2. *Mixing the Concrete*

Measure 9 level tablespoons of the cement into the pie plate. Make a ditch in the middle of the cement and measure 3 level tablespoons of water into it. Now use your old spoon to mix the cement with the water. Add 3 more tablespoons of water (this makes 6 in all) and mix again. Now you are ready to add the sand. You will need *about* 18 level tablespoons of sand. The exact amount depends on how thick your mixture gets. If it is soupy,

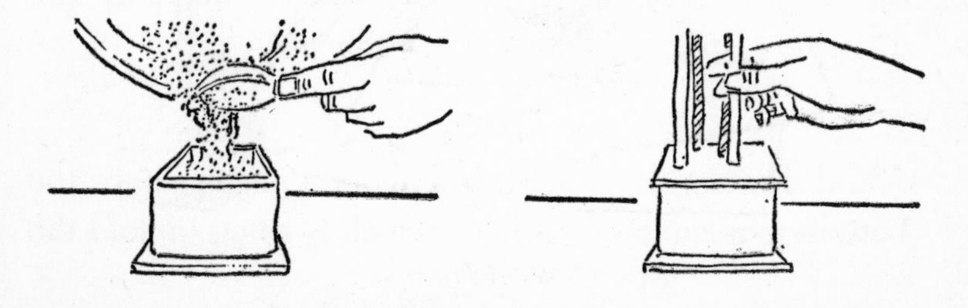

you need more sand. If it is like thick cooked oatmeal (before you add the milk), then you have enough. If it is dry and crumbly, you have too much sand. As you measure in your sand with the tablespoon, continue mixing with the old spoon. Make sure that no dry spots are left.

3. Pouring the Concrete

Spoon the concrete into the box that you made. (Leave one spoonful over and smear it thin on a piece of newspaper, so that you can look at it later.) Now measure your pencils along the outside of the box. Raise or lower them so that they will go about 1 inch into the concrete when the top is placed on the box. Smear some oil on the pencils, so that the concrete will not stick to them. Now place the cover, with the pencils, on top of the box. Push the pencils into concrete.

Clean up! Wash everything that you have used so that the concrete will not harden on these things. Place your box in a quiet place and allow it to dry *thoroughly*. You will have to be very patient, as this should take two or three days. When it is ready, remove the pencils and carefully tear the carton from the concrete. Paint the concrete, if you wish to, with any kind of oil paint. When the paint dries, your paperweight–pencil holder is ready to be used.

MAN-MADE ROCK

In making concrete, you were really copying what nature does in the making of rock. Let us see how. First look at the smear of concrete which you saved from your work. Do you see many grains of sand of different sizes? Do you see how these grains are held together in a hard, dry, gray crust? The gray crust between these grains is cement. It is this cement which hardens and glues all the grains of sand together.

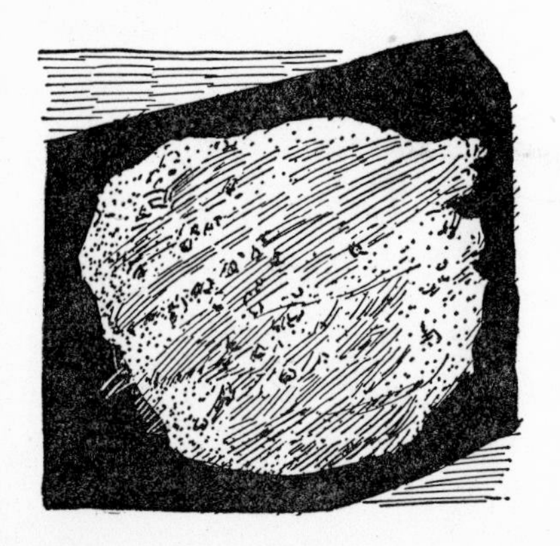

Now if you look carefully at some natural rocks, you will see that some of them are built in the same way as concrete is. These rocks are made of grains and pebbles held together by a cementing material. Long before man began his own rock making, nature was mixing sand, pebbles, stones, and cement with the water in the ground. These hardened slowly into large masses of solid rock.

The cement that man uses is a mixture itself—of different kinds of rocky materials like limestone and clay. These rocks are blasted from quarries and then crushed into a very fine powder. The mixture of limestone and clay is then heated in a hot oven, called a kiln, for a few hours. After cooling, the cement is packed in paper or cloth sacks and is ready to be shipped. All over the world, these hundred-pound sacks of powdery cement are being opened by workingmen. With this cement, these men are building fence posts and water tanks, sidewalks and skyscrapers, highways and bridges, canal locks and dams.

ROCK WHERE WE WANT IT

Before cement came into everyday use, men had to drag heavy stones to make buildings and bridges. The discovery of cement made it possible for man to make his stone where he needed it, and the size and shape he wanted it.

Pouring a house is a new way of using cement, but the use of cement for building goes back thousands of years. The Romans long ago used cement in building monuments, aqueducts, and the walls of buildings. Many of these are still standing, and some of the cement roads made by the Romans 2000 years ago are still used today.

Standing up against wear and tear, wind and rain, heat and cold, this man-made stone is truly a "Rock of Ages."

Glass—A Window on the World

Did you ever wish that you could go back, back, back through the years of history to a time long before your great-grandparents were born—to the time when people lived in caves and wore animal furs for clothing? Did you ever wonder how you could tell these people of olden times about our world of today? What, for example, would you tell them about something they had never seen before, like glass?

Would you explain to them how they might close the opening of their caves with something which would keep out the wind and the cold and yet allow light to come in?

Would you tell them of looking glasses in which they could see themselves as others see them?

Would you tell them of magnifying glasses which make flies look as big as dogs?

Would you tell them of telescope lenses which make the moon seem to be within walking distance?

Would they believe you? Would they understand how glass gives us so many wonderful windows on the world?

FROM SAND INTO GLASS

Now travel forward quickly through time to the world of today, because there are many things about glass that you will want to discover for yourself. First you will want to know how glass is made. It is hard to believe that anything as beautiful and clear as glass is made from ordinary sand. You will find it easier to believe if you scatter a little white sand on something dark, like the cover of a book, and hold it under a light. Do you see many bright, twinkling grains, looking like specks of glass? That is exactly what they are! Look at your sand more carefully with a magnifying glass. You will see that hundreds of the grains are as clear as glass. You will also see many white grains and a few orange and black ones.

How can all these grains of sand be joined together to make glass? Before you answer this question, try another one. How could you make ten ice cubes into one solid piece? There is more than one way of doing this, but the easiest would be to put them all together in a pot and let them melt into water. Then you would pour the water into the ice-cube tray (first removing the separating form) and freeze it again. You would have done the job by *heating,* to melt the pieces together, and *cooling,* to harden them into one solid piece.

Glass is made by heating and cooling, too. Much more heat is needed, however, for melting sand than for melting ice. Ice melts at room temperature, but sand melts at a temperature much hotter than is ever used in your kitchen oven. In order to make sand melt more easily, two other chemicals are mixed with it in the glass factory. These are washing soda (which your mother may use to make cleaning easier) and limestone (which is what chalk and sea shells are made of). These chemicals also become part of the glass and help make it harder and stronger.

The mixture of sand, washing soda, and limestone is cooked together in a clay furnace for about twenty hours,

until clear melted glass is made. To understand how this hot glass can be made into useful things, try these experiments:

BEND IT — SEAL IT — BLOW IT

For these experiments you will need a few eye droppers. Buy the large kind that are sold for about two for a nickel in five-and-ten-cent stores. The heat needed to melt the glass will be supplied by your kitchen range, burning with a low flame. *Hold the eye dropper by its rubber bulb in all these experiments.* Remember that the other end of the dropper is going to get hot, but you have nothing to worry about if you hold it by its bulb.

1. Bending Glass

Place the glass end of the eye dropper into one of the little flames in the outer circle of your range. Hold it so that the flame cuts across the part of the eye dropper just where the glass begins to narrow down. You will see the glass turning an orange-red color. Now take the eye dropper out of the flame and look at it. Has the tip begun to bend? Put it back in the flame and let it bend a little more. Take it out and look at it again. You have made a curved eye dropper. You were able to do this because the heat melted the glass. The melted glass than bent into a new shape.

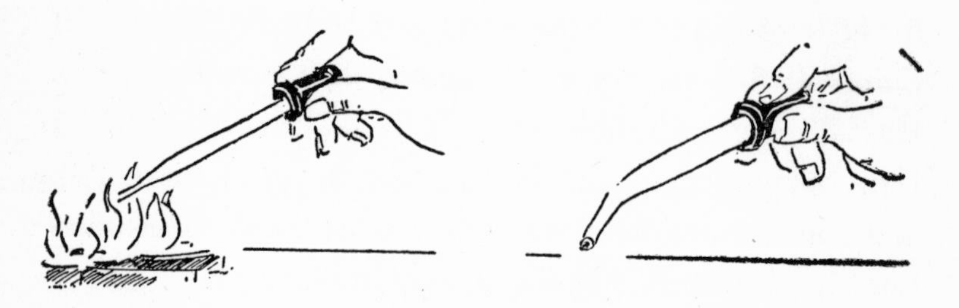

2. Sealing Glass

Now let us see how we can close up the end of the eye dropper. Take the curved dropper that you just made and hold it, curve down, so that just the *tip* of it is in the flame. Take it out of the flame and look at it every ten or fifteen seconds. Is the hole closed? You can prove that it is by first allowing the dropper to cool, and then squeezing the bulb. If no air comes out, the dropper is sealed. In this experiment you have seen how heat melted the glass together and sealed the hole.

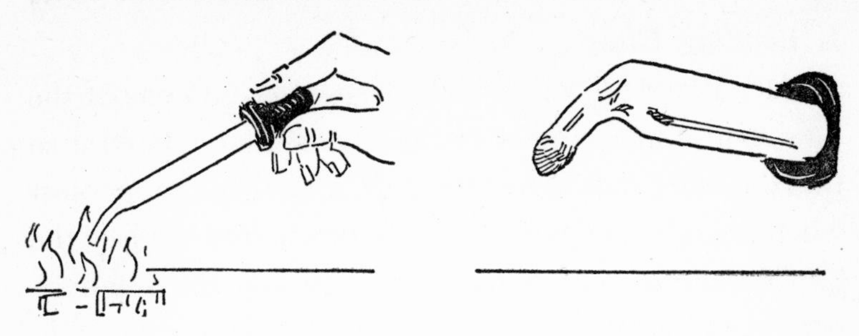

3. *Blowing Glass*

You have blown soap bubbles. How would you like to make a glass bubble? This is the hardest job of all, and you may spoil a few eye droppers before you succeed. Place the tip of your sealed eye dropper in the flame until it becomes red hot. Now remove it from the flame and pump air into the tip by squeezing on the rubber bulb. Has a little glass bubble formed? If you want to make it a little bit bigger, reheat the tip, take it out of the flame, and squeeze again. If you squeeze too hard, your glass bubble may break, just like a soap bubble.

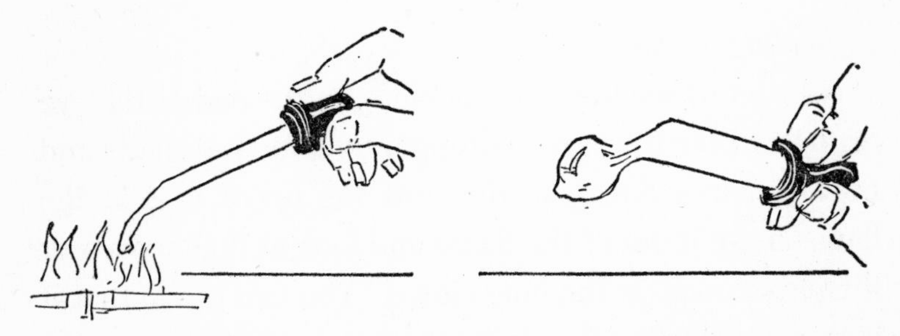

You have bent glass, sealed glass, and blown glass. Now let us go back to the glass factory, to see how they work with glass.

MAKING THINGS OF GLASS

The hot melted glass in factory furnaces can be changed into useful glassware in three different ways: blowing, pressing, and rolling. If you blew some glass in the eye-dropper experiment, it will be easy for you to understand how this is done in the factory. If you didn't, just think of how you blow soap bubbles. In the factory, a man called a glass blower uses a hollow iron pipe about 5 feet long. He sticks one end of this pipe into the melted glass and removes a ball of it. He then puts the other end of the pipe to his lips and blows air into the glass until it swells into a bubble of the right size and thickness. This glass bubble is still soft, and its shape can be changed. If, for example, it is a bottle that the glass blower is making, he puts the glass bubble into an iron form shaped like a bottle. He then blows some more until the glass takes the shape of the iron form. The iron pipe is then carefully

cracked off from the glass. The bottle is taken out of the iron form and is allowed to cool slowly.

For many hundreds of years all blown glass was made by these puffing men. Nowadays ordinary glass bottles are blown by air-pumping machines. Fine glassware, however, is still blown by mouth.

A second way of making glassware is by pressing. Let us see how something like a glass bowl could be made by pressing. Melted glass is poured into a container which is shaped like a bowl. A plunger is then pressed into the glass, forcing it against the side of the container. When the glass cools, the plunger is taken out, leaving a hollow bowl. This way of making glass objects is like putting some soft clay in a bowl and using your fist to press it against its sides to give it the shape of the bowl.

A third way of making things of glass is by rolling. This is a good way to make flat glass, like the kind in your

windows. A long iron bar, held level, is dipped into the melted glass. When the bar is lifted up, the glass sticks to it and is drawn up in a flat sheet. The glass then passes through a row of rollers, like those in a clothes wringer, and a long sheet of flat glass comes out. This glass can then be cut into the sizes needed for windowpanes, picture frames, and other things.

AS OTHERS SEE YOU

There was a time, a few hundred years ago, when mirrors were so expensive that many people never really knew what they looked like. You know how different it is today. How many mirrors are there in your house? Count them

all, large and small—the pocket mirrors, shaving mirrors, bathroom mirrors, and full-length mirrors.

How do mirrors work? Mirrors are usually made of glass with a thin coat of silver on the back. But even clear glass can be a mirror. You prove this to yourself every time you look at your reflection in a store window. Just how can you see yourself? To understand how this is possible, think of light itself. Light can *travel* through space. Light can *bounce* like a ball when it strikes certain objects. Let us now see how this traveling and bouncing of light makes it possible for you to see yourself. Light travels from the sun and strikes your face. Some of this light bounces off and hits the window. Some of the light hitting the window takes a second bounce and travels back to your eye. Here it forms a picture of you.

A mirror, then, is a light-bouncer. Although clear glass can be a mirror, it is not a very good one. It is confusing to see the real things which are on the other side of the glass, together with your own reflection. You can correct this fault, and make an interesting mirror for yourself, by placing a piece of black paper behind a piece of ordinary glass.

A thin coat of silver behind the glass is best of all, because silver is a much better bouncer of light than glass. As you look into a good silvered mirror, you sometimes think that you are looking into another room with people and furniture in it. You feel, as Alice did, that you could step right "through the looking glass."

TO SEE THE VERY SMALL

Hobbies sometimes lead to discoveries. Take, for example, the hobby of Leeuwenhoek (lay′-ven-hook), who lived in Holland about 300 years ago. His hobby was

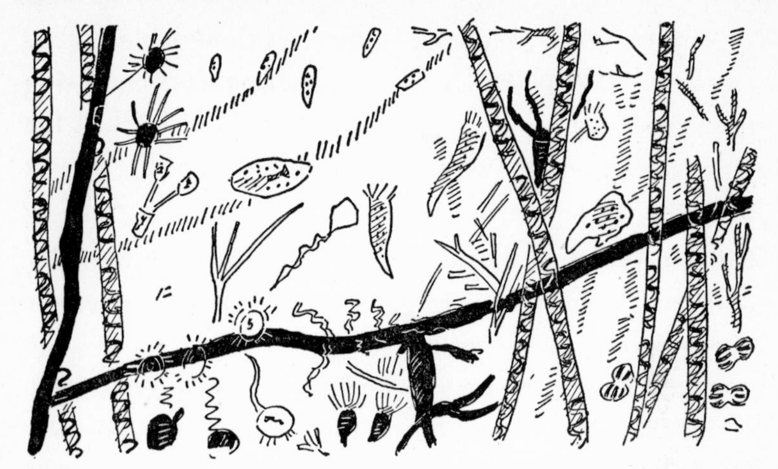

grinding and polishing small pieces of glass. He worked on these pieces until he had shaped them into powerful magnifying glasses. (Special glasses like these, and others found in eyeglasses, telescopes, and cameras, are called lenses.)

So carefully did he do his work, that his magnifying lenses were stronger and clearer than any that had been made before. Leeuwenhoek looked at everything he could get hold of with his new lenses—the stinger of a bee, the tail of a fish, the leaf of a plant, a drop of milk, and many other things. One day he placed a little drop of pond water under his magnifying glass. To his great surprise, he found that this drop was filled with thousands of tiny plants and animals. He had discovered a new world of living things which had never been seen before.

What makes a magnifying lens magnify? Is it because it is made of a special kind of glass? Or is there another reason? You can find out by making a lens yourself.

You Will Need:

a piece of newspaper
a glass of water
a toothpick or a broom-straw
a saucer
a bit of kitchen fat

In this experiment you are *not* going to use glass to make your lens. Instead you are going to use something which allows light to pass through it and can easily be shaped to make a lens. Can you guess what it is? Ordinary water!

Make a thin smear of fat on the newspaper to cover a space about the size of a penny. Be sure that a letter "o" is covered by the fat. Now dip the toothpick into the glass of water. Let a drop run off the toothpick onto a letter "o" of the print. Notice that the water does not soak into the paper, because the water and fat do not mix. Notice also that the water has formed a little round drop. Now look through this drop at the letter "o." Does this "o" look bigger than an "o" which is not under water? You have made a magnifying lens out of water!

Is it the water itself that does the magnifying, or is it something about the shape of the water drop? You can find the answer by tearing out the piece of greased newspaper and putting it in the center of the saucer. Now pour enough water from the glass into the saucer to cover the paper with a layer of water about 1/8 inch high. Now look at the print. Does it look any bigger than the print on a piece of dry newspaper?

When the water was in the shape of a curved drop, it made the print look bigger. When the water was in a flat layer, the print remained the same size.

It's all in the curve! And what is true for your water lens is also true for glass lenses.

Lenses have many uses. Teams of lenses working together in powerful microscopes help us see tiny objects that our eyes alone could not see—things like bacteria and the red cells in blood. Lenses in telescopes make faraway stars appear closer to us. Lenses in cameras help make pictures on the film. Lenses in eyeglasses make the world clearer for millions of people.

SPECIAL KINDS OF GLASS

Did you ever place a cold milk bottle in a sink and run hot water on it? Did it crack? This is one of the faults

that ordinary glass has, but we have found out how to prevent this. A few years ago some railroad men asked a glass company to make a new kind of glass chimney for the trainman's signal lantern. They wanted a kind of glass which would not crack, even when the hot lantern was taken out into the rain or cold. A young scientist working for the glass company discovered how to make this kind of glass. He mixed boric acid (which is sometimes used as an eyewash) with the other materials used in glass-making. This new heat-resistant glass was found to be good not only for lanterns, but for kitchen baking dishes.

Another kind of glass made auto traveling safer. The glass in the windshields of automobiles is now made like a sandwich—two pieces of glass are the bread, and a clear rubbery material is the filling. When this glass is struck a heavy blow, as it might in a crash, it will crack, but the pieces will stick to the rubbery material and not fly out.

How is colored glass made? If you look at a piece of window glass though its edge, you will notice that it has a green color. This color is caused by a small amount of

iron in the glass. We have found that we can make glass of any color by mixing different chemicals with the materials that are used in glassmaking. When nickel is added, a purple glass is made; copper makes it green; gold makes it red.

A few hundred years ago, glass windows, bottles, and drinking glasses were so expensive that few people could afford to have them. Today these things are cheap in price, but you know that glass is more useful to man than gold.

Rubber—Jack-of-all-trades

Rubber is a Jack-of-all-trades. See all the things it can do for you:

A rubber ball *bounces* high.

A rubber band *stretches,* but *snaps* right back when you let it go.

A rubber raincoat *sheds water* and keeps you dry.

A rubber balloon *holds air* until you allow it to escape.

A rubber eraser *wears away* as it picks up pencil marks, but the tough rubber in an auto tire *lasts* a long time.

A rubber covering on electric-lamp wire *keeps electricity away* from your fingers.

A rubber cement *glues* things together.

No wonder that we use rubber to make thousands of useful things. But where does it all come from?

MILKING TREES

Long before the rest of the world learned how to use rubber, the American Indians were making things out of it. On one of his trips to America, Columbus discovered that the Indians were playing games with rubber balls. They also made water jars and shoes from rubber. How did the Indians get their rubber?

By milking trees! First the Indians would make a number of slanting cuts through the bark of the rubber tree. At the lower end of each cut they would hang a small cup. Milky drops oozed out of the cuts and dripped into the cups. How did the Indians make this white, watery stuff, which we now call latex, into dry, hard rubber?

DIP AND SMOKE

Let us see how they would make a rubber shoe. First they would model some clay or mud into the shape of their own foot. Then they would dip the model into a jar of latex. When the model was lifted from the jar, a thin coating of latex stuck to it. This was then held over a smoky fire until the water was dried out of it, leaving a thin coat of dry rubber. The dipping and smoking was repeated many times until the shoe was thick enough. Then the clay model was washed out of the rubber and the shoe was ready to wear.

Would you like to make something out of latex? Of course the first thing to do is to get hold of some latex. Ordinarily, you can buy a small amount of latex (a half pint will be enough) by writing to any of the large rubber companies in the United States. There are times, however, when there is a shortage of natural tree latex. If you find this to be true now, you can still buy man-made (synthetic) latex from some of the rubber companies. This kind of latex can be used in the experiments that you are going to do, except that you will have to first add some ordinary salt to it.

DRY IT OUT

First let us see how we can dry some latex into rubber. Dip the tips of your fingers into the jar of latex. Now rub the drops between your fingers until they are dry. The small bits left on your fingers are pieces of rubber. Roll them together into a tiny ball. Throw the ball on the table. Watch it bounce. You have made dry rubber from milky latex in the Indian way, except that you have used the heat of your fingers instead of a smoky fire to dry out the water. Finger drying, however, would be a slow, sticky way to harden a large amount of rubber. And a smoky fire isn't a pleasant thing to have around the house. There is an easier way to do the job.

QUICKER WITH VINEGAR

You Will Need:

an eye dropper
three drinking glasses
water
vinegar
latex

Pour some of the latex into a glass. Half fill another glass with water. Pick up a drop of latex with your eye dropper and let it fall into the glass of water. Notice how the latex spreads through the water, making it milky. But we want to harden rubber; we don't want to spread it. How can we do it?

Your nose is going to help you. Smell your latex. Do you smell ammonia? This ammonia was added to the latex soon after it was collected at the rubber plantation.

There was a good reason for this. Latex is like real milk in many ways. You know that if milk is allowed to stand outside the refrigerator for some time it will turn sour. This souring makes the milk curdle into little lumps. Fresh latex does the same thing. If it is allowed to stand, it too will sour and curdle. At the plantation, therefore, some ammonia is added to it. This preserves the latex by preventing the souring and curdling. (If you are using man-made latex, you will not smell ammonia. This is because another kind of chemical is used as a preservative.)

But now you *want* to harden the rubber, you *want* it to curdle. Then you will have to get rid of the ammonia. You will have to make the latex sour. How can this be done?

You can find the answer by reading the label on a bottle of household ammonia! This label tells people what to do in case some of this strong ammonia (which we are *not* going to use in our experiments) gets into their eyes, or their mouths, or spills on their skins. You see that it tells them to use different things like vinegar, lemon juice, grapefruit juice, orange juice, or boric acid to fight the ammonia and get rid of it. Notice that all of these ammonia fighters are sour, acid things. Let us use one of these, vinegar, in our experiment, to get rid of the ammonia and to make the latex sour.

Half fill a glass with vinegar. Pick up some latex with your eye dropper. Drop some into the glass of vinegar. What happens? Do you see that the latex has curdled into a little white ball? Take it out of the vinegar. Squeeze and roll it in your hands until it is dry. Throw it on the floor. Watch it bounce. You have made rubber from milky latex by hardening it with vinegar. In factories where rubber things are made from latex, it is hardened in the same way.

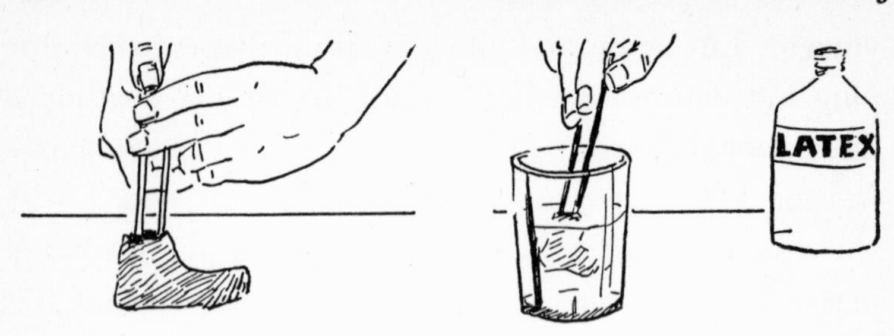

MAKING THINGS FROM LATEX

Now you are ready to make something from latex. Perhaps you would like to make a tiny rubber shoe, or a toy hot-water bottle or rubber tire. Use the same materials that you just experimented with. You will also need some modeling clay and two thin sticks. Wooden lollipop sticks will be fine for this job.

First make your modeling clay into the shape of the object that you want. Then push the sticks into one end of it, so that you can handle it easily, and not have to put your fingers in the latex or the vinegar.

Now dip your clay model into the latex until it is completely covered. Lift it out and allow the extra latex to drain off. Now dip the latex-covered model into the

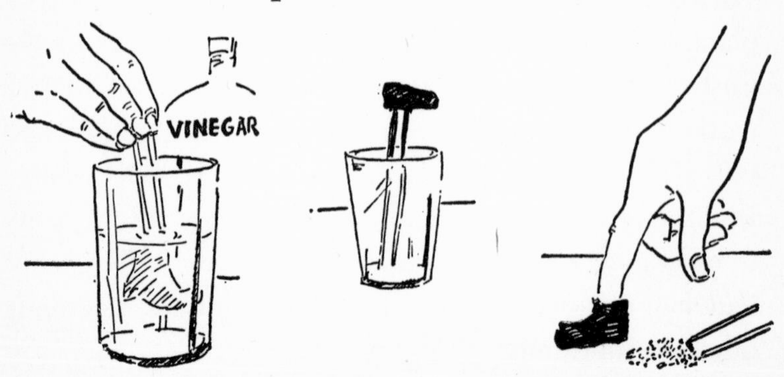

vinegar. Lift again and allow to drain. Repeat this dipping into latex and vinegar until the rubber coating is thick enough to suit you. Now comes the hardest part—waiting for the rubber to dry. Place your work on its sticks in an empty jar for a few days until the rubber is perfectly dry. Be sure that the rubber is not touching the sides of the jar, as it may stick. When the rubber is dry, remove the sticks and dig out the modeling clay.

PLANTATION TO FACTORY

Have you ever broken the stem of a milkweed plant? If you have, you saw the sticky white stuff that came out of it. This is real latex too, but there isn't enough of it to make it worth while for men to use it in rubber making. However, if you get a chance to gather some milkweed, see if you can make a small amount of dry rubber, using what you have learned in your experiments to help you do the job.

Latex is made by hundreds of different plants, but most of the world's supply is gathered from the hevea tree. This tree, which first grew in Brazil, is now grown on plantations in many of the islands and countries in the Eastern Hemisphere. The latex is gathered by native workmen and brought to a mill. Here it is either hardened into slabs of crude rubber, or preserved as milky latex. In either form, it is shipped to rubber factories far away to be made into golf balls and rubber heels, bathing caps and floor mats, conveyor belts and rubber rafts, and many other useful things.

Wool – Fleece for Man

Apes and bats, bears and beavers
Cats and dogs, foxes, goats
Mice and rabbits, sheep and woodchucks
Warm and snug in furry coats.

Bareskinned man is not so dumb, though,
He knows how to use his brain
To borrow wool from Mother Nature
And clothe himself from cold and rain.

Blankets, carpets, gloves, and jackets
Mufflers, mittens, and pajamas
Shirts and stockings, suits and sweaters
He learns his lesson from the llamas.

HEAT PRESERVER

When we think of wool we think of . . . cozy, comfortable warmth. Do woolens really keep us warmer than other materials? Let us see by doing a simple experiment.

You Will Need:

hot water
3 small, covered jars
1 woolen sock
1 cotton sock

Fill the three jars to the top with hot water and cover them tightly. Wipe the outside of the jars dry. Now pull the woolen sock around one jar, covering it as if it were your foot. Pull the cotton sock over the second jar. Leave the third jar as it is. Place all three jars in a cool place. After about a half hour, remove the socks and feel all the jars. Which is the warmest? The coolest?

You will find that wool keeps its jar warmest. Now think of your own body. It is warm, like a jar of heated water. Of course you don't have to heat your body over a stove to make it warm—it is making its own heat inside.

Now if this heat is lost from your skin faster than your body makes it, you *feel* cold. This is where clothing comes in. The wool in your clothing and in your blankets keeps you warm because it *prevents* the heat which your body is making from escaping too quickly. Wool is a heat preserver.

A BLANKET OF AIR

Why is wool better than other materials for keeping us warm? You can find the answer by doing this experiment.

You Will Need:

- a piece of woolen cloth, 2 inches square, cut from an old piece of clothing
- a piece of cotton material, 2 inches square, cut from an old sheet
- 2 drinking glasses
- a pencil
- water

Half fill each of the glasses with water. Push the piece of wool cloth to the bottom of one glass with a pencil. Remove the pencil. Does the wool float to the top? Can you guess why? Now push the wool under again and keep it on the bottom. Do you see large bubbles of air popping out of the cloth and rising to the top? Does the woolen cloth finally stay at the bottom without holding? Now try the same experiment with the cotton material. Does it have to be held under? Do bubbles come from it?

The dry wool had a lot of air trapped in it. You forced the air out when you "drowned" it. The secret of wool's

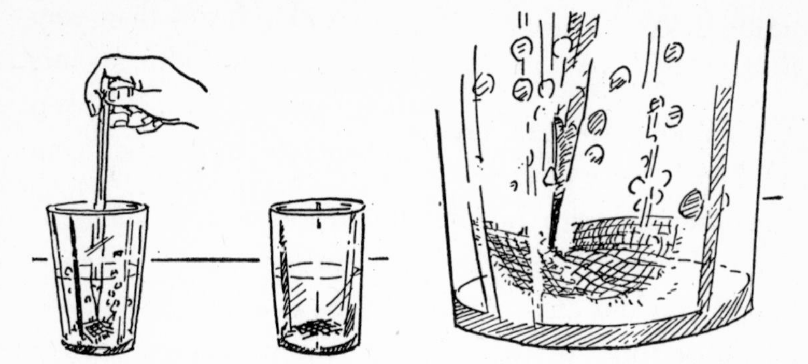

warmth is in this *trapped air*. It may surprise you to know that the reason that woolens keep us warmer is that their fibers trap and hold a layer of still air around our bodies. This quiet, motionless air is better than almost anything else for preventing the heat from leaving our bodies. So when you buy a good blanket or a good sweater, you are really buying a good air trapper.

Birds have their own built-in air trapper—their feathers. In cold weather, they fluff their feathery coats to trap more air in them. This keeps them warmer. In building houses we also use trapped air in the space between the inner and outer walls. This air space prevents the heat of the house from escaping too quickly in the cold winter. It also stops the heat outside from coming into the house in the hot summer.

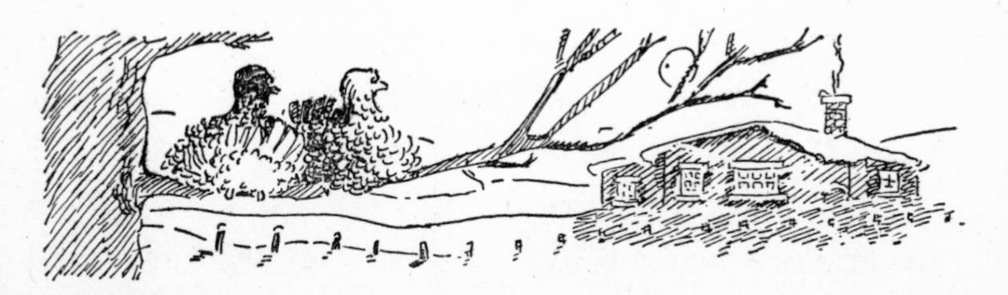

STRETCH AND SPRING

There is another important reason why wool is so good for clothing. You can discover this by holding one end of a 12-inch piece of knitting yarn in one hand, pulling on the other end with the other hand, and then letting go. It jumps like a rubber band! It is springy in another way, too. If you look at your yarn closely, you will see that it is made of three or four thinner strands twisted around each other as in a rope. Untwist a piece of yarn until all these strands are straightened out. Now let go. You will see that the strands jump back into their old twist, just like a spring.

This springiness of wool is important in all the clothes made from it. In the first place, it makes woolen clothing feel comfortable on you because it can stretch to take the shape of your body. In the second place, it prevents wrinkles from forming easily; when some do form they are "sprung" out. In the third place, it keeps things like woolen blankets fluffy; they do not flatten out. And, as you remember from your experiments, this fluffiness keeps you warm because of the trapped air.

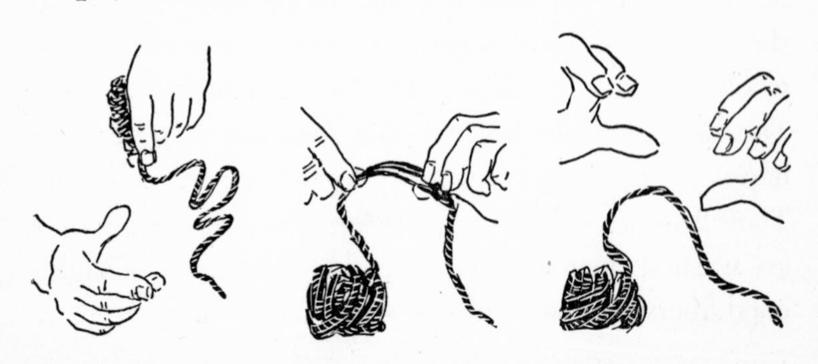

FROM THE SHEEP'S BACK

Now that we know why wool is so useful, let us go back to the animals which grow the wool and see how their fleeces are made into yarn. In a quick trip around the world you would find alpacas, llamas, and vicunas in South America, camels in Africa and Asia, Angora goats in Asia Minor, Cashmere goats in northern India and Tibet, and sheep almost everywhere—all serving as wool-growers for man.

If you were to visit a sheep ranch in Montana in April or May, you would be there in time for the shearing of the sheep. The heavy coat of wool which the sheep have been growing all year is ready to be cut. Two sheep shearers usually work together on one animal, cutting the woolly fleeces with shears which look like hedge clippers. The sheep are not hurt by this shearing, but they are happy to scamper away, back to the open ranch land. Their fleeces are packed and shipped to a mill. Here they are washed clean and combed into flat bands of straightened fibers. The wool is now ready for spinning.

PULL AND TWIST

How can the wool fibers, which average only 6 inches in length, be spun into yarn hundreds of feet long? You can find the answer by doing some spinning yourself. All you need is a pair of hands and a piece of knitting yarn. Since this yarn is already spun, you will have to unspin it to get the wool fibers. To do this, begin at one end of the yarn. First untwist about 1 inch of the yarn. You will see that it is made of three or four thinner strands. Now pull out the small threads *in* each strand, catching them between your thumb and forefinger. The smallest thread that you see is a wool fiber. Work your way down, an inch at a time, until you have pulled all the fibers out of the yarn. Now the spinning begins.

Hold the ball of tangled wool fibers that you just made in one hand. Pull some of them out and twist them together with your other hand. Keep pulling more fibers and twisting them into your yarn, until you have used all of them. You have now spun yarn out of wool fibers.

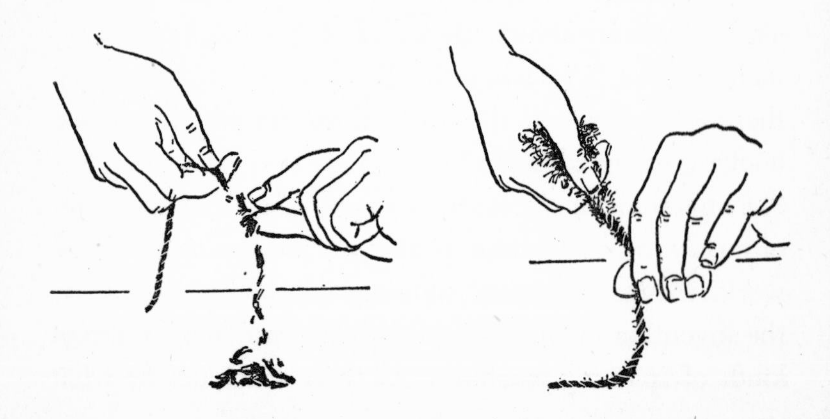

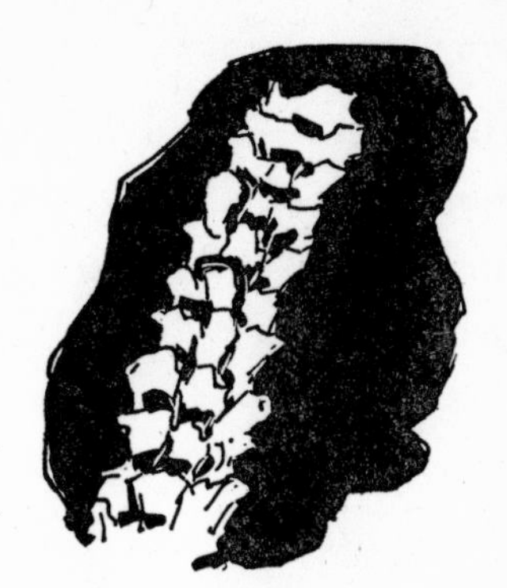

Your yarn may not be as trim and as strong as the piece you began with. This is not surprising, however, when you remember that you had to work against the old twist, and that you had to work with shorter fibers. You have seen how short pieces of fiber can be twisted into a long yarn. What makes these pieces stay together? Why don't they pull apart? Well, for one thing, the twisting itself helps lock the fibers together. But there is another reason which is to be found in the wool fiber itself. If you could look at a single wool fiber under a powerful microscope, you would see it is covered with tiny scales, like those on a fish. There are about a thousand of these scales on every inch of fiber. Now when the fibers are twisted together, these scales catch on the scales of the neighboring fibers, hooking them together.

People long ago spun their yarns by hand. As a matter of fact, yarn is still spun in this way in some parts of the world. Faster and easier spinning was made possible by the invention of the spinning wheel, and later, different kinds of spinning machines. All these machines do what

you did—they pull out the fibers and twist them together. From the spinning machines the yarns are sent to the weaving machines to be made into many different kinds of woolen materials. You can understand weaving best by doing some weaving yourself.

SHUTTLING THROUGH

How would you like to weave a piece of woolen cloth on a loom? You can do it easily with the things you have in your home. You can make your own loom from a piece of cardboard. You can then string the loom with a set of supporting yarns. Then you will be able to weave crosswise into these yarns to make a piece of woolen cloth.

You Will Need:

- cardboard (3 inches square)
- 2 small balls of knitting yarn of different colors
- scissors
- ruler
- pencil
- darning needle

1. Making the Loom

Cut a 3-inch square of cardboard. The kind found on the backs of some writing pads is good. Rule a line ¼ inch from one end of the cardboard. Now rule another line, ¼ inch from the opposite end. Make a row of dots ¼ inch apart on each of these lines. If you have done your work carefully, you should have eleven dots on each line. Now cut slits with the scissors from the edge of the cardboard to each of the dots. You should now have twelve teeth at each end of the loom.

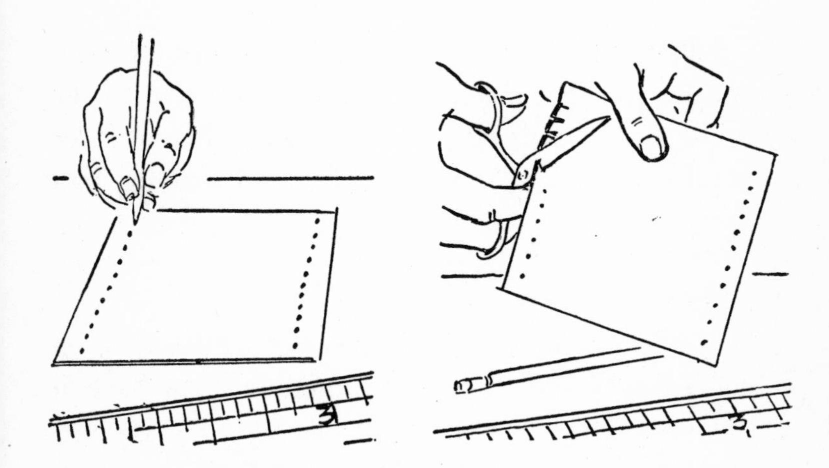

2. Stringing the Yarn

Place your yarn through the first slit on the top left corner of the loom, leaving a short end sticking out of the back. Now lead the yarn across the front of the loom to the first slit on the opposite end. Run the yarn through the slit, around the back of the tooth to the next slit, and then bring it out to the front. Now run the yarn up to the second slit on the opposite end. Repeat what you have just done, going up and down the front of the loom until you reach the last slit on the top.

Allow a short piece of yarn to stick out of the back. The yarn that you have just strung is called the warp.

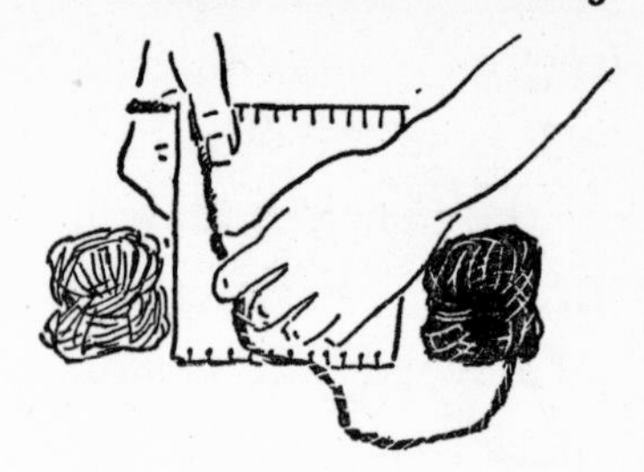

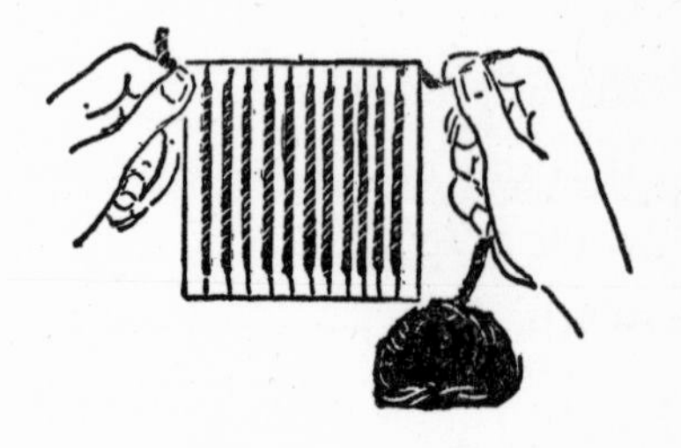

3. Weaving

This is an over-under-over-under job. Thread the yarn (using another color) through your darning needle and cut off a piece that is not too long to work with (about 2 feet). If you do not have a suitable darning needle, you can make one out of a piece of cardboard, like the one in the picture. This large needle is called a shuttle, because it shuttles back and forth across the warp. Lead your yarn through the warp, using an over-under-over-under weave. When you reach the end of the line, go *around* the last warp thread and weave your way back. You will notice that your second row is under the warp wherever your first row is over it. Continue in this way, weaving

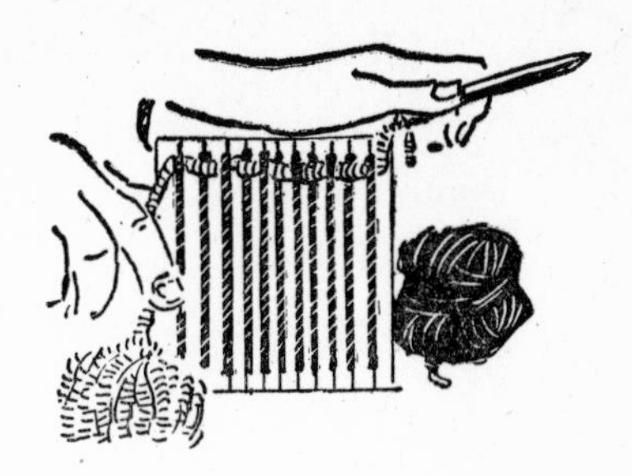

back and forth. If you need a second piece of yarn, rethread your needle and start where the first thread ended. It is not necessary to tie the two pieces together. If you want a tight weave, push your threads together along the warp.

The wool that you have just woven into the warp is called the woof. When you have finished your weaving, remove the cloth from the loom by pushing the loops of the warp off the teeth.

You have just woven a piece of *homespun* cloth. People have been weaving cloth like this for thousands of years, shuttling woof through warp, just as you did. A few inventions made the work easier and faster. You can understand these inventions if you think of some of the troubles you had while weaving. Wouldn't it have been

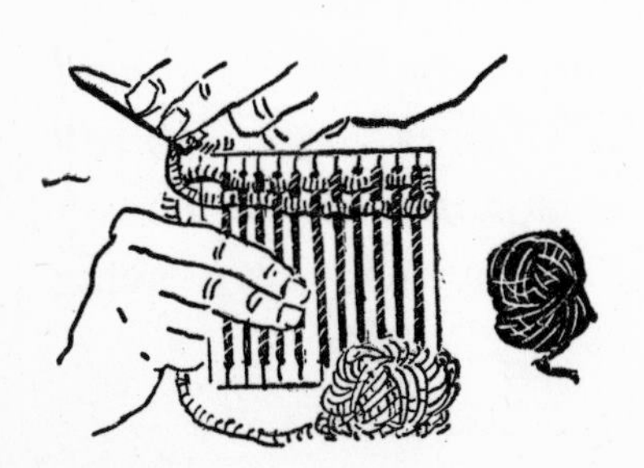

easier if all the warp yarns that your needle had to pass under could have been lifted up at the same time? In this way you could have passed your needle through easily, in one straight push, instead of having to weave over and under. On the return trip, the other set of warp yarns could have been picked up, and your needle could have skipped right back. Long ago, a bar called a harness was invented to lift one set of yarns while the shuttle went through. On the return trip this harness was lowered, and another harness lifted the other set of yarns. This invention is used today on all looms.

Another invention which made weaving faster was the weaving machine, which is driven by electric or steam power. In this machine the harnesses are lifted at just the right time, while the shuttle is shot back and forth so fast that you can hardly see it.

When people of olden times first began to clothe themselves against the cold and the rain, they used the skins of animals and leaves of trees and grasses. When some curious men found that they could twist and weave the woolly fibers of animal fur into clothing, they started mankind on the road to a more comfortable and more healthful way of life.

Salt—The Spice of Life

Shake some salt on a piece of colored paper. Look at the small grains with a magnifying glass. Do you see hundreds of glistening objects which look like tiny ice cubes? These are crystals of salt. The reason that salt sprinkles so nicely is that it forms these separate tiny crystals. Put a few drops of water on these grains of salt. Do you see the crystals disappearing before your eyes? They are dissolving into the water, making it salty like ocean water.

Salt is very plentiful. There is enough salt in the waters of the oceans to cover the United States with a layer of solid salt a mile and a half thick. There are also great deposits of salt buried in the earth.

SALT AND YOU

What good is salt? You know that meat and string beans

taste better when you add a pinch of salt to them. But do you know that your body needs this salt? If you have ever licked a drop of blood from a cut in your finger, you probably noticed that it tasted salty. Your blood needs this salt in order to serve your body properly. But why must you keep on eating salt? If you lick the back of your wrist you will find the answer. Your body is always losing salt in your sweat. Salt is also lost from the body in your urine. All this lost salt must be replaced. Men who work in hot places like foundries or mines sometimes suffer from a condition known as heat cramps because they have lost too much salt in their sweat. Such workers are now given salt pills to prevent this from happening.

Animals need salt too. If you have ever visited a farm, you have probably seen the large blocks of salt which farmers place in their pastures for their cows to lick on. Deer and many other wild animals will travel many miles to a natural salt spring or a salty rock.

IN THE DAYS BEFORE REFRIGERATORS

Salt was very important in another way in the days before refrigerators were used. Can you guess why? The following experiment will give you the answer.

You Will Need:

2 teaspoons of chopped beef

½ teaspoon of salt

2 jars

2 labels

Mix a teaspoon of chopped beef with ½ teaspoon of salt. Place it in a jar. Now put a teaspoon of chopped beef in another jar. Do not put salt in it. Label the first jar MEAT WITH SALT and the second jar MEAT WITHOUT SALT. Cover both jars and place them on a shelf in your closet. Look at them every day for a week. What do you see? What do you smell?

Foods spoil because of the work of millions of tiny bacteria in them. Salt kills the bacteria, thus preventing them from decaying the food. However, the meat that is kept in your refrigerator does not have to be salted, because the cold in there prevents the bacteria from becoming active. Because of this the meat will be preserved for a number of days. In the deep-freeze refrigerator, however, foods can be kept for months and even years without spoiling. Although the refrigerator has taken over most of salt's old job, salt is still used as a preserver of certain fish and meats.

GETTING SALT OUT OF THE OCEAN

Many years ago, people learned how to get salt out of the ocean. They trapped some of the ocean water which flowed over their coasts into long, shallow ponds. When these ponds were dried up by the hot sun, salt was left at the bottom. Would you like to get some salt in this way?

You Will Need:

1½ level teaspoons of salt	a large plate
a drinking glass	a saucepan

Even if you don't live near the ocean, you can make something very much like ocean water by stirring 1½ level teaspoons of salt into a glassful of water, until all of the salt dissolves and disappears. Then pour half of the salt water into the plate and place it outside in the sun. If it is winter, place the dish on a radiator.

But you are in a hurry! Well, pour the rest of the salt water into a saucepan and heat it slowly on your kitchen stove. When there is just a little water left, turn the heat down as far as possible. Watch carefully now, so that you do not burn the saucepan or the salt. When all the

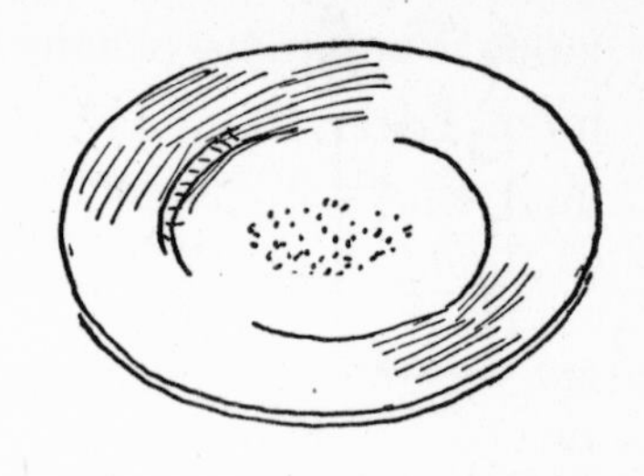

water is gone, turn the heat off. Wait five minutes for the saucepan to cool off. Do you see a white crust on the bottom of the saucepan? Scrape it together with a spoon and place it in a small saucer. Taste it. Sprinkle some on a piece of bread and butter and eat it.

Some time later, look at the plate of salt water. What has happened? Do you find salt here, too? You have gotten salt from your homemade ocean water.

SALT FROM THE LAND

Most of the salt which we use today is not taken from the ocean, but from large salt deposits in the earth. One way to get the salt out of the earth is to dig it out in much the same way as we dig for coal. Another way is to drill a deep hole through rock to the salt buried underneath it. A pipe is placed in this hole, and fresh water is pumped down through it to the salt below. Some of the salt dissolves in this water. The salty water is then pumped up through another pipe. The water is then boiled away by heating it as you did in your experiment, and the salt remains.

Where did these salt deposits come from? Millions of years ago, salty oceans covered much of what is now dry land. When these oceans dried up, they left their salt behind. Later these salt deposits were covered by sand, mud, and pebbles which hardened into rock.

SALT FOR OTHER JOBS

Have you ever seen men sprinkle salt on icy sidewalks or roads? Do you know why they do this? You can find the answer by experimenting with ice and salt.

You Will Need:

2 ice cubes
2 cups
½ teaspoon of salt

Place each of the ice cubes in a separate cup. Pile the salt on top of one of the ice cubes. What is happening? Which ice cube is melting faster? Is the top of the salted ice cube sinking?

Salt makes sidewalks and roads safer because it can make ice melt even when it is freezing outside.

Man has put salt to many other uses. More salt is used in the making of other chemicals than any other material. Salt is used in the making of DDT, the new chemical which is used to kill harmful insects. Salt is important in the making of glass, pottery, soap, and hundreds of other things which the early American Indians never dreamed of when they called salt the "magic white sand."

Bread – The Staff of Life

Do you enjoy eating a good slice of bread? So do millions of people all over the world. All of these people know how to grind the seeds of certain plants into a powdery flour. They know how to mix this flour with water to make a pasty dough. They know how to bake this dough into a tasty bread. Would you like to make some bread from seeds?

FROM SEEDS TO BREAD

You Will Need:

- ¼ cup of wheat seeds (Buy ½ pound from a grain or feed store. Save what you do not use for other experiments.)
- a rolling pin
- a small baking dish
- a dab of butter
- a meat grinder
- a dough board

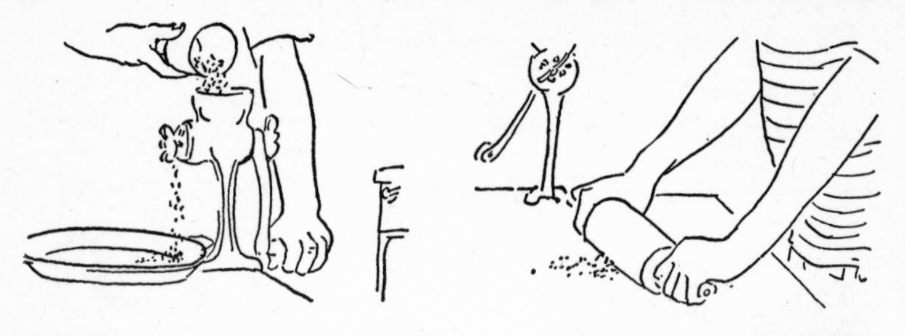

Grind the wheat seeds through the meat grinder seven or eight times. Do you have a fine flour yet? Probably not. Then place your chopped wheat in the center of your mother's dough board. Get to work with the rolling pin, crushing the wheat into as fine a flour as you can get.

You are now ready to make the dough. Place 5 or 6 teaspoons of water in a cup. Add your flour to it slowly, stirring all the time. When you have a thick, pasty mixture, you are ready to bake. Smear a little butter in the baking dish. Spoon the dough into it and bake it in the oven until it is brown. Let it cool. Taste it. Spread butter on it. Eat it. You have made bread from wheat seeds! This is the kind of bread that was made thousands of years ago, before people learned how to make it light and spongy.

Not all bread is made from wheat.

The Mexicans make bread from corn.
The Indians of Asia make bread from peas.
The Chinese make bread from rice.
The Europeans make bread from rye.
Some of the American Indians used to make bread from acorns.

But all of these breads are made from the dried seeds of plants.

WHITE FLOUR AND BROWN FLOUR

Look at some store-bought flour. This is wheat flour, but it is much whiter than the kind that you made. Can you guess why? You can find the answer by studying a single wheat seed.

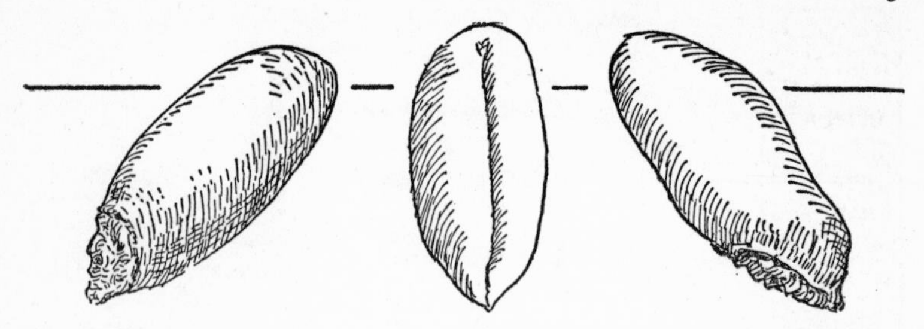

You Will Need:

1 wheat seed	a magnifying glass
a pair of pliers	a piece of paper

Look carefully at the wheat seed. You can see it better if you look at it through a magnifying glass. Do you see a small, wrinkled part near one end of the seed? This is called the germ. You will find out later what the germ is. Do you see the yellow-brown covering of the seed? This is called the husk. Now crush the seed with the pliers, letting all the bits fall on a piece of paper. What do you find? Do you see the white, powdery material which comes from the inside of the seed? Separate some of the white stuff from the rest of the seed and push it to one side of your paper. This is white flour. The rest of your seed is husk and germ.

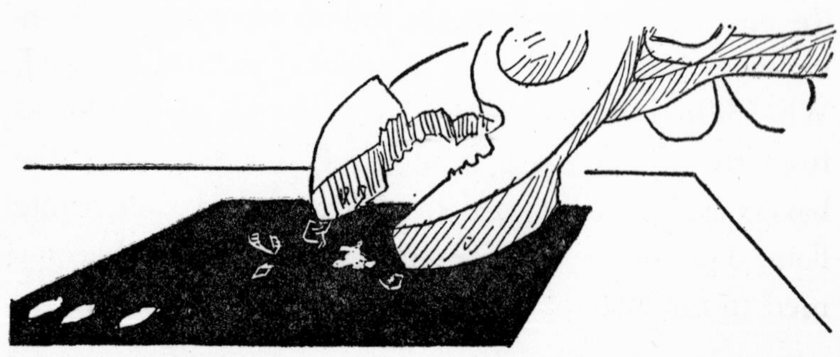

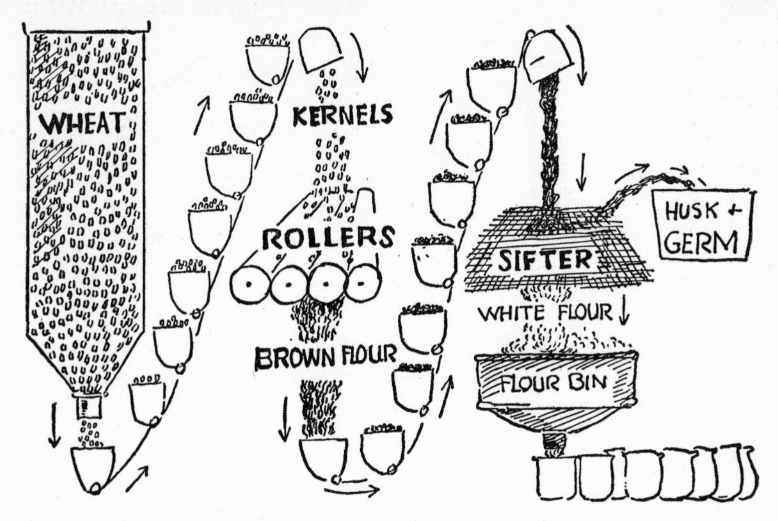

The white flour that you buy in grocery stores is made in large flour mills. Here the milling machinery separates the husk and the germ of the wheat seeds from the white flour. Only the white flour is sent to the breadmakers to be used in making the kind of white bread that most Americans eat today.

A number of years ago, some scientists found that the husk and the germ of the wheat plant contained valuable vitamins, minerals, and proteins which were not in the white flour of the inside of the seed. This meant that in the making of white flour, the millers were really throwing away some of the most nourishing parts of the seed. Why didn't we decide then to make all of our bread from the whole wheat seed? Well, for one thing, the bakers had become used to making bread from white flour. For another, the American people had become used to the taste of white bread. It was not so easy to

change old habits. The government, however, wanted to improve the bread eaten by the American people. It got the bakers to agree to add some of the missing minerals and vitamins to the white flour. This enriched flour gave us a more healthful bread.

Not all the wheat bread that is sold is white bread. Graham bread, for example, is made from the whole wheat seed, just like the bread that you made. Whole-wheat bread, despite its name, is not made from the whole seed. In making the flour for this kind of bread, the coarser part of the husk is removed.

FROM SEEDS TO PLANTS

The germ of the wheat seed which you looked at before contains a baby wheat plant. Would you like to see it grow?

You Will Need:

12 wheat seeds
a bowl
a plate to cover the bowl
a clean blotter

Line the bowl with a wet blotter. Place the seeds on the blotter. Cover the bowl with a plate. In a day or two the seeds will begin to sprout. Add water if your blotter becomes dry. Do you see a stem and roots growing out of the germ of each seed? The rest of the seed is giving food to this young plant until it is big enough to make its own food. Do the plants look like grass? This is no accident, because wheat is a kind of grass. If you want your wheat plants to keep on growing, you will have to plant them in soil, and see that they get sunlight and water.

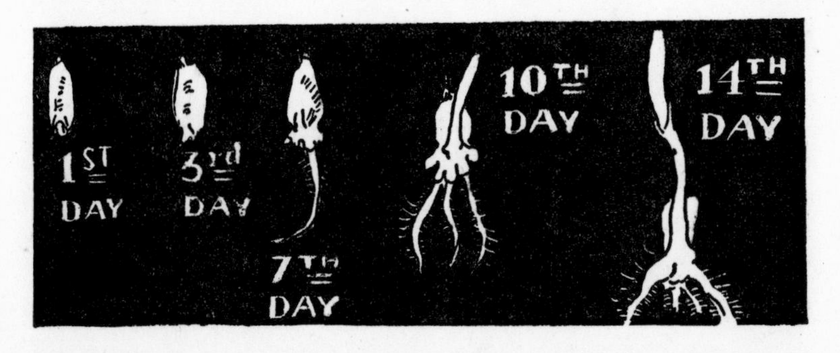

WHY BREAD IS FULL OF HOLES

Look at a slice of bread. You will notice that it is full of small holes. Hold it in your hand. See how light it is. The bread that you made in the first experiment was much heavier and did not have the spongy look of store-bought bread. Why is there this difference? You can find the answer by making two kinds of bread.

You Will Need:

The materials listed below are needed for *each* of the two breads you are going to make.

½ cup of flour
1 teaspoon of sugar
1 cup
1 saucer
butter
1 custard cup or any other small baking dish

For *one* of the breads only, you will also need ¼ teaspoon of dried yeast.

1. Bread with Yeast

Mix the flour and sugar in a saucer. Place 5 teaspoons of lukewarm water in a cup and stir the dried yeast into it until the water becomes milky. Now add the flour-sugar mixture, a little at a time, to the yeast water and mix thoroughly. Continue doing this until you have made a pasty dough. Now smear butter on the inside of your baking dish and put your dough into it.

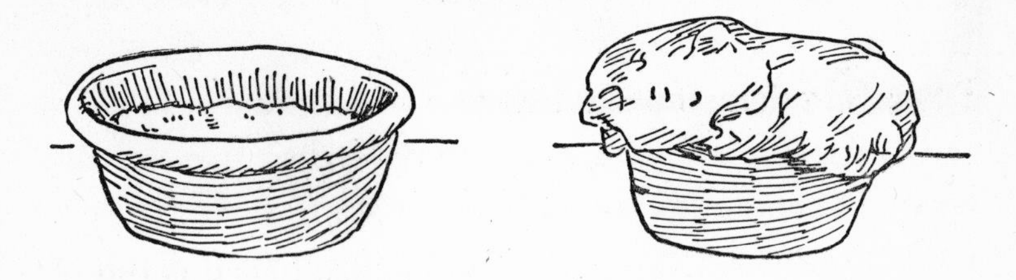

2. Bread without Yeast

Prepare another batch of dough in the same way, but this time do *not* put any yeast into the lukewarm water.

Cover both dishes with a clean cloth. Look at them every fifteen minutes. What is happening? Which one is rising? Do you see hundreds of tiny bubbles in one of your doughs?

When the yeasty dough has doubled its size, you are ready to bake. Place both dishes in a heated oven. When the two breads are brown, take them out of the oven and allow them to cool. Cut each of them in half. How do they look? How do they taste?

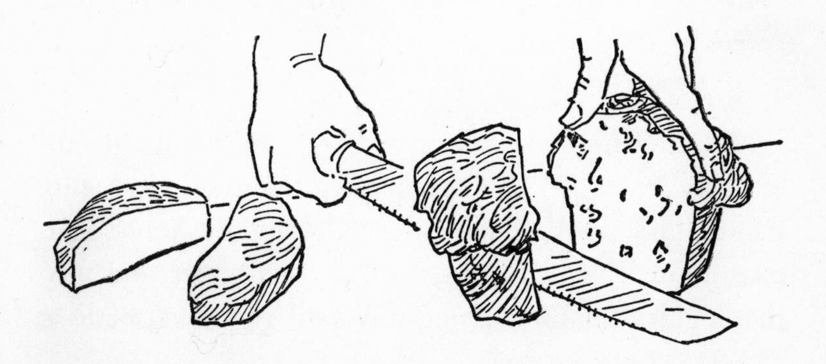

The yeast seems to make all the difference! How does it work? In the dried yeast that you mixed with the lukewarm water there were thousands of tiny plants, which are too small to see unless you look at them through a powerful microscope. When you added flour and sugar to the yeast water, you were really feeding these plants, causing them to become active and start growing. While using the food, the yeast plants gave out large amounts of a gas called carbon dioxide. This is the same gas that makes bottled soda bubbly. These thousands of carbon dioxide bubbles blew up your dough and made it rise. When you baked your bread, the heat made the bubbles still larger. The dough rose higher. Finally the dough formed around each of these bubbles, making a light, spongy bread.

So you see that two plants are used in breadmaking: wheat, whose seeds supply the stuff for bread, and yeast, whose bubbles make it light and tasty. If this bread contains all the good things found in the whole wheat seed, it is a wonderful, healthful food for all peoples. It is their staff of life.

Soap – Dirt Chaser

Sparkling faces, fresh clothing, shining dishes, clean floors—this is our way of life. This is the way that makes for good looks and good health. When we think of cleanliness we think of water and soap. Does soap really help clean things? Or would plain water do just as well?

SOAP ON THE JOB

Let us find the answer to these questions by watching soap at work. The "dirt" in this experiment is oil.

You Will Need:

2 drinking glasses
toilet (hand) soap
2 pieces of cotton material (1 inch square)
2 pieces of brown paper
a teaspoon of oil (salad oil will do)
a cup

Half fill two glasses with warm water. Mix a small piece of soap in *one* of them until you have made a lot of suds. Then pour a teaspoon of oil into a cup. Soak the two pieces of material in the oil to make them "dirty." Then take them out and squeeze all the extra oil out of them. Unfold the pieces and sink one of them into the soapy water and the other in the plain water. Allow both pieces to remain in the water for about eight minutes. Then take them out to see how well the oil has been cleaned out of them. You will find this easy if you use an oil detector. Do you know what an oil detector is? Just an ordinary piece of brown wrapping paper!

Rub each piece of material on a piece of this paper. Allow the paper to dry for a few minutes. Now hold the paper up to the light. Do you see that the material that was in plain water has left a large, greasy spot on the paper? Do you see that the other piece has left only a small spot of grease, or no spot at all?

You have just seen that soap helps clean the oil out of some cotton material. Just *how* did it do it? How does soap help clean things?

BREAK IT UP

To find the answer to this question, try another experiment with soap, water, and oil.

You Will Need:

- toilet soap
- a few drops of oil
- a toothpick or matchstick
- an eye dropper
- a cup
- a drinking glass

Clean a drinking glass thoroughly with soap and warm water. Then rinse it four or five times with warm water to make sure that *all* the soap is out of it. Now half fill the glass with warm water and let it stand for a minute, to give the water a chance to become quiet. Pour a small amount of oil into the cup. Pick up some of the oil with your eye dropper and then let two drops of oil fall into the glass of warm water. If you have done your work carefully, you should see a round spot of oil floating on the water.

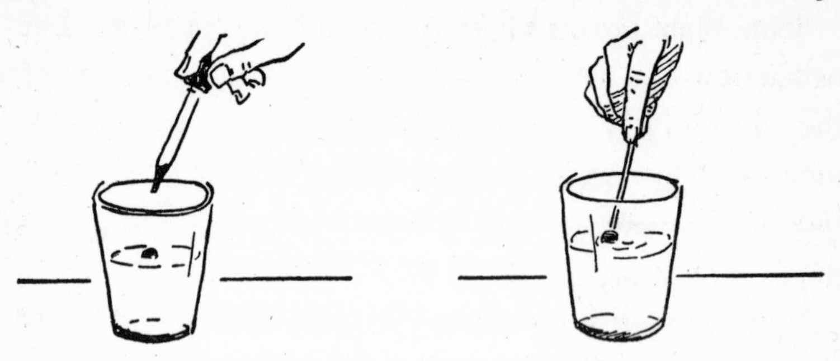

Now take your stick and poke it gently into the drop of oil. Spin the drop of oil around. Push it around. Try to break the drop into smaller ones. You find that this is not easy to do. Even when you do break the drop, the little drops that are formed join together again into one large drop.

Now coat the end of the stick with soap by rubbing it against the bar of soap. Watch carefully now, because you are going to see something very exciting. Put the soaped end of the stick into the center of the oil drop. Did you see the drop of oil spread out over the water? Did you see it being dashed against the side of the glass and breaking into a number of smaller drops? See if you can break some of the smaller drops in the same way.

Soap, then, breaks big drops of oil into small ones. Let us see how this helps in cleaning. Think for a moment of the oil sticking to the cotton material in the first experiment. In soapy water the large drops of oil on the material were broken into small ones. These small drops popped out of the material into the soapy water.

Soap helps clean things in other ways, too. If you have stepped on a bar of wet soap in the bathroom you know how slippery soap can be. This slipperiness helps in sliding the dirt off soiled dishes, clothing, and hands.

GREAT-GRANDMOTHER MADE HER OWN SOAP

Soap was one of the things that used to be made at home. This was a good place to do it, because the stuff needed for soapmaking—the ashes from burnt wood, and fat—was right there. All winter long the fats from cooking and the wood ashes from stoves and fireplaces were carefully saved. In the spring, the whole family helped in the soapmaking.

The wood ashes, together with some straw and lime, were dumped into a barrel. Every few hours, a pail of water was poured into the top of the barrel. The water, wood ashes, and lime together made a new chemical called lye. (Nowadays lye is sometimes used in the home to clean stopped-up drainpipes.) This lye dripped out from a hole in the bottom of the barrel into a pail.

The lye and the fat were then boiled together in a large iron kettle. When great-grandmother decided that the soap was finished, the fire was allowed to go out. In a day or two, the soap hardened in the kettle. It was then cut up into bars which were used until the next soapmaking time came around again.

THE WONDERS OF CHEMISTRY

Soap, then, is made from lye and fat. It is really wonderful that strong lye and greasy fat can make pleasant, cleansing soap. It is wonderful that when chemicals are mixed together something new is made. But this kind of a change, called a chemical change, is an everyday happening. It happens when milk turns sour. It happens when iron turns to rust. It happens when yeast acts on the sugar in bread dough to make bubbly carbon dioxide gas. It happens in your body, too, when the food you eat is changed into muscles and bones.

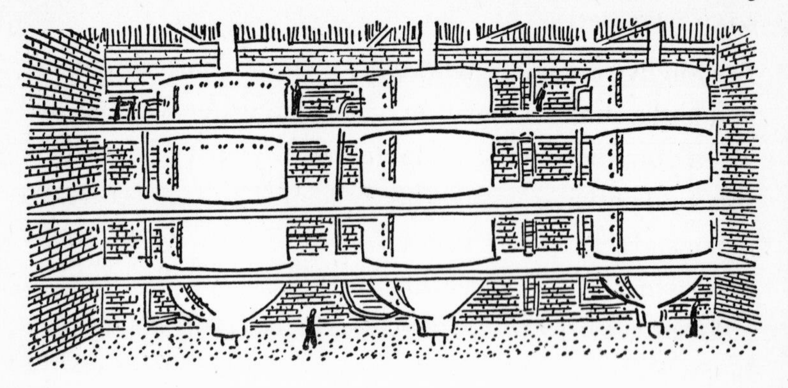

A BIGGER KETTLE

Nowadays soap is made in factories. Here the mixture of fat and lye is boiled in giant kettles. Some of these kettles are as high as a three-story house. Steam pipes in the bottom of these kettles heat the mixture until it boils and bubbles like a volcano.

Today many different kinds of fats and oils go into the making of different kinds of soap:

Tallow, the fat from beef
Lard, the fat from hogs
Coconut oil, from the coconut
Palm oil, from the fruit of the palm tree
Cottonseed oil, squeezed from the cotton seed
Soya bean oil, from the soya bean
Olive oil, from the olive

These fats or oils are boiled with the lye for two or three days in the giant steel kettles. Then the soap is pumped out of the kettle into other machines. Here it hardens into bars, flakes, or tiny granules.

SOAP'S WEAKNESS

Do you live in a place where the water is "hard"? Or have you had a summer vacation where the water was "hard"? Then you know what happens when you try to wash in this kind of water with ordinary soap. The soap refuses to make suds. It doesn't clean well. It forms a white, sticky curd which stays on clothing and dishes.

What is hard water? How does it get hard? First, let us begin with rain water, just after it has fallen from the clouds. This kind of water makes good suds with soap. It cleans well. It does not leave a sticky curd on dishes and clothing. As a matter of fact, people living in hard-water places treasure this kind of water so much that they put out barrels to catch the rain water which runs off from their roofs. This kind of water is called "soft" water.

But rain water usually has to take a long trip before it reaches your faucet. Sometimes it soaks through the soil and runs on the underground rocks. In some of these rocks there are certain minerals which are carried away by the running water. When water has a large amount of

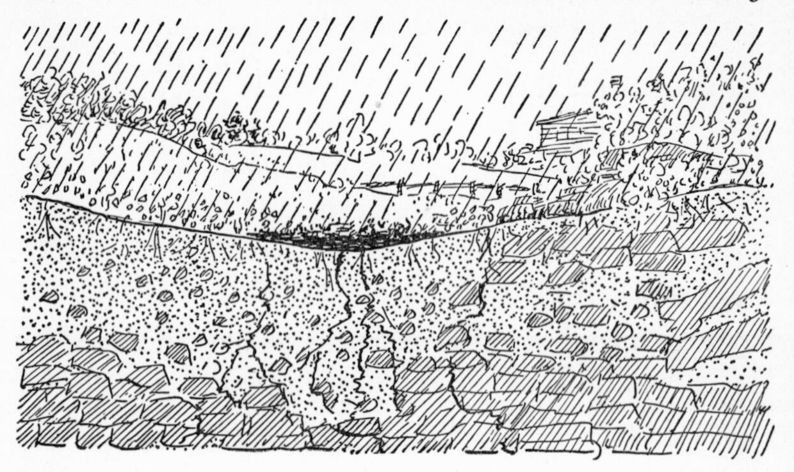

these minerals in it we call it "hard." You cannot see the minerals because they are dissolved in the water in the same way that salt is dissolved in sea water. But you *can* see what these minerals do to soap.

Let us take a close look to see what hard water does to soap. For this experiment you will need hard water and soft water. If you live in a hard-water region, fresh rain water will be your soft water. If you don't live in a place where there is hard water, you can make some by using Epsom salts, because this is one of the minerals that makes water hard.

You Will Need:

2 drinking glasses
2 teaspoons
Epsom salts (½ teaspoon)
soap flakes or granules

Half fill two glasses with warm water. Mix ½ teaspoon of Epsom salts into the water of *one* glass until all of it has dissolved and disappeared. This is your hard water. The other glass has your soft water. Now mix ½ teaspoon of soap into *both* glasses, using a separate spoon for each glass. Try to make suds in each glass. In which one can you do it?

Stop mixing, and allow the water in each glass to stand for a few minutes. Do you see that you still have suds in the soft water? Do you see that no suds have formed in the hard water, but that instead a thick white curd has collected at the top of the water?

Now empty both glasses into the sink. Look at the empty glasses. The soft-water glass is fairly clean. The hard-water glass has a white ring inside of it.

Hard water, then, makes no suds when soap is mixed with it. Instead it curdles the soap into a sticky curd. This happens because the minerals in hard water join with the soap to make something new—curd. This is another example of a chemical change, but this time it is working against us.

What can be done about this? How can people living in hard-water regions get good suds? There are a number of ways of doing this. One way is to take the minerals out of the water by adding certain chemicals to it. Another way is not to use ordinary soap at all! Let us see how this soapless way works.

SOAPLESS SOAP

Old-fashioned soap now has a younger brother. This younger brother is sometimes called "soapless soap" or "synthetic detergent" (sin-thet′-ik dee-tur′-gent). It is called "soapless" because it is not made from fat and lye like ordinary soap. It is an entirely different kind of chemical, but it does the same job as old-fashioned soap, and in some cases it does it better. Let us experiment to see how soapless soap works in hard water.

You Will Need:

- soapless soap (synthetic detergent)
- Epsom salts
- 2 drinking glasses
- 2 spoons
- granulated or flaked soap

Make hard water in *both* glasses by mixing ½ teaspoon of Epsom salts into ½ glass of warm water. Stir ½ teaspoon of soapless soap into one glass. Stir ½ teaspoon of ordinary soap into the other. Try to make suds in both. Then stop stirring and allow the water to stand for a few minutes.

Do you see that the soapless soap has made a good sudsy mixture? Do you see that the ordinary soap has made no suds, and that a white curd has collected at the top of the water?

Now empty both glasses into the sink. The glass which had soapless soap in it is sparkling clean, except for a few bubbles. The other glass has a white ring sticking to it.

Ordinary soap, then, joins with the minerals in water to form a curd or film which sticks to clothing and dishpans. This film must be rinsed away. Soapless soap, on the other hand, is not changed by the minerals in water. It does not form a curd. There is no sticky film to be rinsed away.

Soapless soap is only one of the many kinds of soap that are made for special jobs. Just look at all the other kinds of soap around your house: toilet soap, shampoo soap, shaving soap, scouring soap, furniture soap, carpet soap, and all kinds of clothes-washing soaps. When we add all of this up, we find that 25 pounds of soap are used each year for every person in the United States.

Paper–A Web for Words

Tear a small piece of paper out of a newspaper. Hold it up to the light and look at it. Do you see hundreds of hair-like threads sticking out of the torn edges? Look at them with a magnifying glass. Tear the little piece of paper into smaller pieces. Do you see more threads? No matter how you tear your paper you will always find these tiny threads—the whole paper seems to be made of them.

Where do these threads come from? If you break a small piece of wood in half (a toothpick will do) and look at the broken edge, you will see tiny threads there too. You can see the same kind of threads in a stalk of celery, a blade of grass, or in a piece of straw. These long, thin hairlike threads are plant fibers.

The threads that you saw in the newspaper are plant

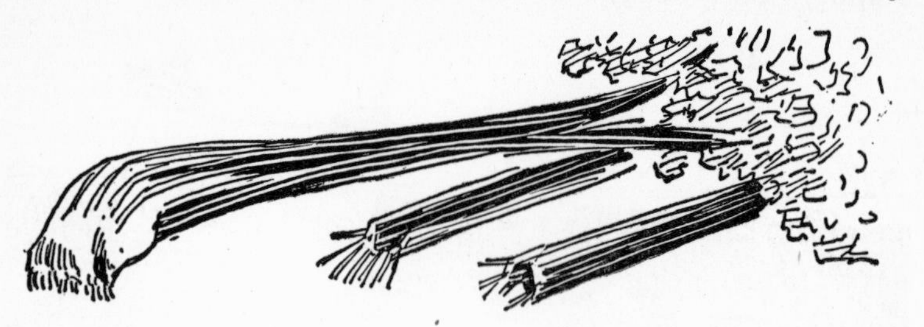

fibers too. All paper—tissue paper, blotting paper, writing paper, wrapping paper—is made of plant fibers. The page that you are reading now is made of about six million fibers!

THE FIRST PAPER – PAPYRUS

About 4000 years ago the Egyptians learned how to make paper from the stems of some grasslike plants that grew along the banks of the Nile. They cut these stems into long flat strips and laid them side by side. They then placed another layer crosswise on top of the first layer. These layers were glued together by the muddy waters of the Nile or with a paste made from flour. The sheets were then rolled flat and allowed to dry in the sun. After drying, the paper was rubbed smooth with shells.

For about 2500 years this kind of paper, called papyrus, was the most common writing material. A new way of making paper was discovered later by the Chinese. Instead of using large strips, they shredded bamboo stalks or cotton rags into tiny pieces. These shreds were then thrown into water and picked up by a sieve to form a sheet of paper. You can understand how this was done by making some paper yourself.

PAPER FROM RAGS

You Will Need:

- a piece of old, white linen (about 6 inches square) from a torn linen towel, tablecloth, or napkin
- liquid laundry starch
- a piece of wire screening (about 2 by 3 inches)
- a rolling pin (a food can will do)
- 2 clean pieces of cloth (muslin)
- a large mixing bowl
- newspaper
- water
- a pair of scissors
- a small saucepan
- a teaspoon of colorless gelatin
- a spoon
- a cup

1. Cut or tear the linen into pieces about 1 inch square. Shred these with your fingers until you have a batch of threads, with no fabric left.

2. Pick up bunches of the threads and cut them into *tiny* pieces with your scissors.

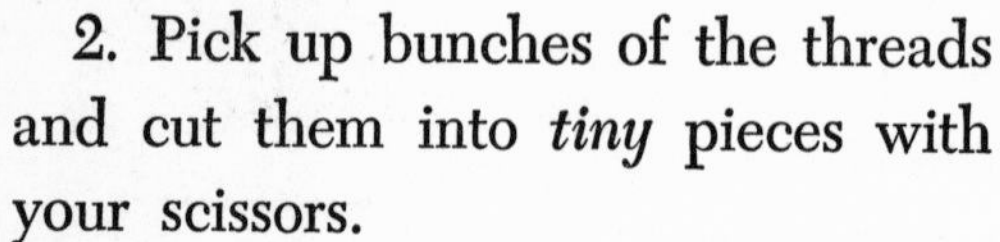

3. Put all the pieces into a saucepan and cover them with water. Boil for ten minutes.

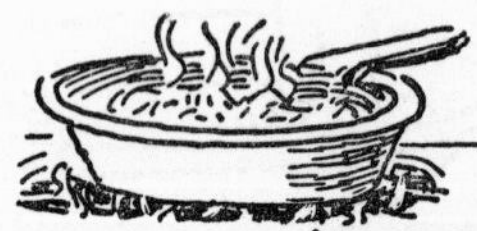

4. While the water is boiling, prepare some starch water by adding 1 cup of liquid laundry starch to about 3 cups of water in the mixing bowl. Stir. If your laundry starch does not have bluing in it, add a few drops to help whiten the paper. Now pour the boiled linen threads into the starch water and stir them up.

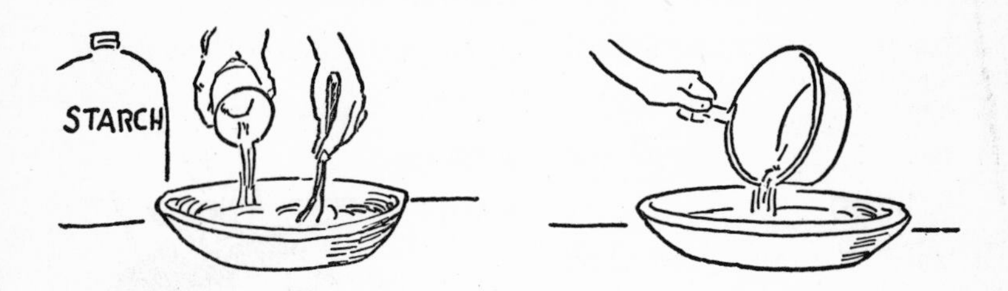

5. Slide the wire screen down along the side of the bowl until it lies on the bottom. Holding it level, lift it straight up slowly. If you have done the job well, your wire screen will be covered with a thick layer of linen threads. If you are not satisfied, dip the screen into the starch water, shake the threads off, and try again.

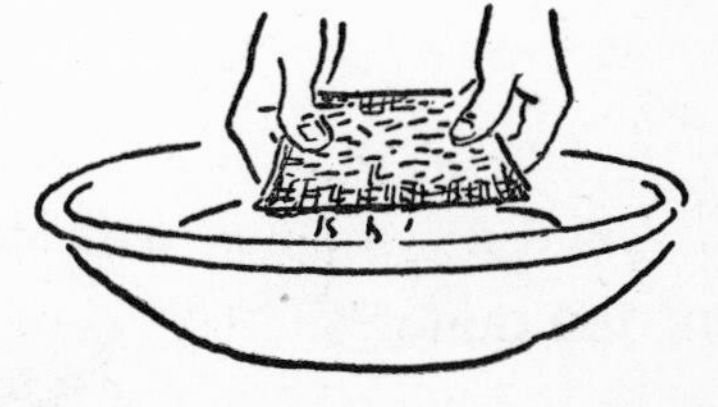

6. Place your screen with its mat of threads on a piece of cloth. Cover with another piece of cloth. Use your roller to squeeze the water out of the threads.

7. Remove the cloth and place your screen with its threads on a piece of newspaper. Now mix 1 teaspoon of colorless gelatin into a few teaspoons of cold water in a cup. When it has dissolved, add enough boiling water to make about ¼ cup. Pour a few teaspoons of this gelatin water on top of your mat of threads.

8. Allow your paper to dry overnight. The next day, remove it carefully from the screen. Trim the edges with a pair of scissors. Write the words LINEN PAPER on it, for this is what you have made.

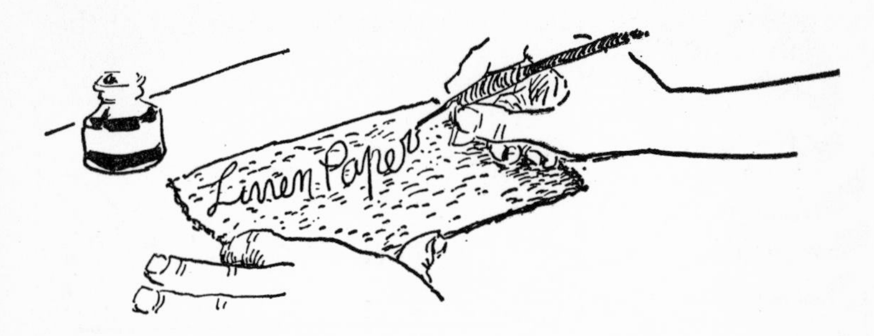

Isn't it wonderful to make a piece of paper with the things you have right in your own home? Now let us take a closer look at what was happening while you were busy at your job.

Your paper was made from plant fibers, although you got them secondhand. Other men had taken these fibers from the stems of the flax plants and had woven them into linen cloth. You shredded this cloth into tiny pieces. These pieces were then tangled together in a flat web. When this web of plant fibers dried, it became paper. Cooking the fibers made them swell and stick together better. The starch helped fill the spaces between the fibers to make an even sheet of paper. Bluing made your paper whiter. The gelatin made the paper smoother and also made it possible to write on it with ink without smearing.

EASIER AND FASTER WITH MACHINES

For many hundreds of years people made paper by hand from cotton and linen rags just as you did. Then, in 1798, a French worker named Louis Robert announced that he had discovered a way to make paper more quickly. He did this with a paper machine. This machine was able to turn out sheets of paper of a very large size, even 12 feet wide and 50 feet long. This kind of machine is still used today, although many improvements have been added. Let us take a close look at a modern paper machine.

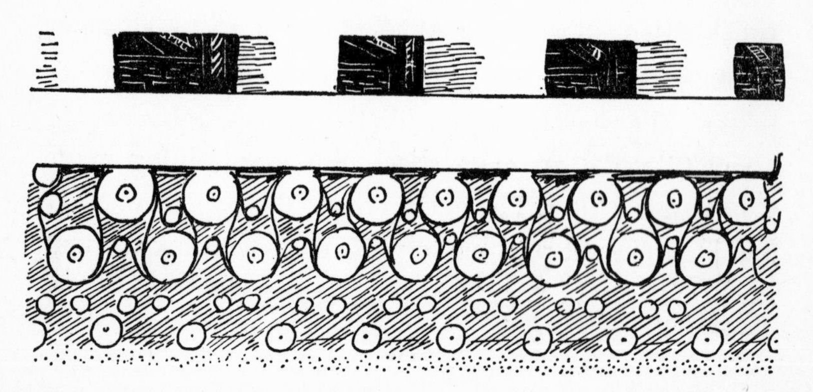

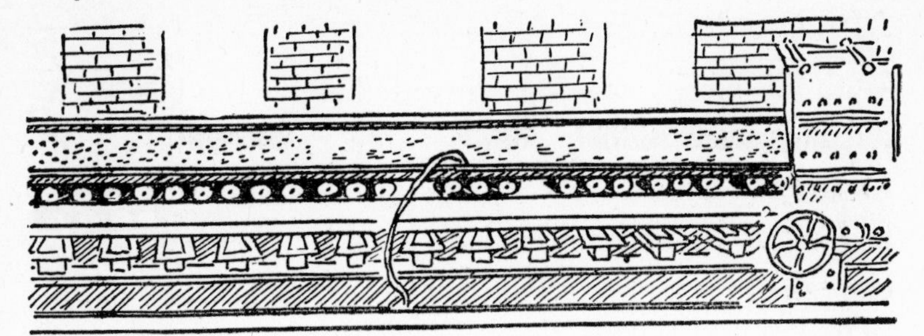

At the beginnning or "wet" end of the paper machine, a mixture of fibers and water are poured from a large tank onto a moving wire screen. This screen has the shape of a long, wide belt which moves all the time, like the chain on a moving bicycle. As the screen moves along, water drains through its many tiny holes, leaving a mat of wet paper. Near the other end of the machine the paper leaves the screen and is picked up by a moving belt of woolen felt. This belt carries the paper through some heavy rollers, which, like clothes wringers, squeeze water out of it. The paper is now strong enough to leave the belt, and it passes through another set of heated rollers which dry it completely. All of this takes place so quickly that some machines make a mile of paper every three minutes!

LEARNING FROM THE WASPS

With this kind of machine, invented about 150 years ago, old rags were quickly changed into clean, white paper. More and more paper was made and used. But this paper-making machine soon led to trouble: there were not enough old rags around to feed the machines. Things got so bad that in 1820 the owners of an American paper mill advertised in the newspapers, begging all young ladies to bring their old rags to the factory so that enough paper could be made for letters from their sweethearts.

A German named Frederic Keller tried to find an answer to the question, "Where can we find more stuff out of which to make paper?" He remembered the words of the French scientist René de Réaumur (ra-nay′ da ray-o-meer′), who said, "The rags from which paper is made are becoming scarce. While the use of paper increases every day, the production of linen remains the

same. The wasps seem to teach us that paper can be made without the use of rags and linen. These wasps invite us to try to see whether we can make fine and good paper from the use of certain woods." Keller decided to watch the papermaking wasps. He saw the females biting little bits of wood and chewing it with their strong jaws into a soft, mushy pulp. He saw them spreading this pulp on their nests in the trees. He saw how this pulp dried into a tough paper which served as a cover for the nests and as cradles for the young wasps. Later in the year he saw how the wasps made their nests larger by cutting away paper from the inside of the nest and building new layers on the outside.

Keller told a friend what he had discovered. This friend, Henry Volter, was a papermaker. They decided to experiment together to see whether they could make paper from wood. After many tries, they finally found that they could change tough wood into a soft pulp by

grinding pieces of it between grindstones and then soaking it in water. With this wood pulp they were able to make a piece of rough paper in 1850. One invention followed another. English and American inventors found that they could make better paper by cooking chips of wood with certain chemicals. The purpose of this cooking was to remove all the other materials from the wood and leave only the pure fibers.

These new ways made it possible to make enormous amounts of paper. It solved the rag shortage problem but started a new one—the shortage of trees. Here in America we have been chopping down trees faster than new ones have grown to take their place. We are only beginning to solve this problem by planting more trees, by protecting trees from fire and from harmful insects, and by setting aside more land for public forests.

This has been a long story—4000 years from papyrus to wood-pulp paper. It has been a United Nations story—inventors from Egypt, China, France, England, the United States, and many other countries, each with their discoveries. It has been the story of man making good use of these inventions to provide himself with paper for wrapping and blotting, for cardboard and wallboard, but, most important of all, for writing and printing. On these white sheets of tangled plant fibers we have been able to save the words and the thoughts of men. Through these printed words one man may speak to another, though they are separated by thousands of miles or thousands of years.

More Adventures Ahead

Right now men and women all over the world are trying to find the answers to many puzzling questions.

Although there are still large amounts of coal and oil buried in the earth, the supply will not last forever. Can we find new ways of making heat?

In many places on the earth, the supply of fresh water for drinking, washing and for growing plants is not large enough. Can we find new inexpensive ways of getting fresh water from salty ocean water?

Chimneys from factories puff large amounts of soot into the air over our towns and cities. How can we prevent this?

New man-made materials like rayon and nylon are

taking the place of wool and silk, but they do not have all the good qualities of these natural materials. Can we make new materials which are as good as, and even better than, wool and silk?

The amount of good soil to grow food crops on is growing smaller. How can we build up the soil to provide plenty of food for all the people of the world? Can we grow large amounts of food plants without soil?

Before you are very much older, these adventurous men and women will find the answers to many of these questions. They will find the answers by looking closely, by experimenting carefully and by thinking clearly—just as you did in your explorations. And some day *you* will be adventuring ahead to answer the new questions of the future.

Index – How? What? Why?

I want to find out HOW:

I want to find out WHAT:

I want to find out WHY: